P9-AOZ-970

A DECLARATION OF THE PEOPLE'S NATURAL RIGHT TO A SHARE IN THE LEGISLATURE

A Da Capo Press Reprint Series

THE ERA OF THE AMERICAN REVOLUTION

GENERAL EDITOR: LEONARD W. LEVY

Claremont Graduate School

A DECLARATION OF THE PEOPLE'S NATURAL RIGHT TO A SHARE IN THE LEGISLATURE

Which is the Fundamental Principle
of the
British Constitution of State

BY GRANVILLE SHARP

DA CAPO PRESS • NEW YORK • 1971

A Da Capo Press Reprint Edition

This Da Capo Press edition of
A Declaration of the People's Natural Right to a Share in the Legislature
is an unabridged republication of the first edition published in London in 1774.

Library of Congress Catalog Card Number 74-119046
SBN 306-71955-X

Published by Da Capo Press, Inc.
A Subsidiary of Plenum Publishing Corporation
227 West 17th Street, New York, N.Y. 10011

Manufactured in the United States of America

A
DECLARATION
OF THE
People's Natural Right to a Share in the Legiſlature, &c.

A DECLARATION OF THE PEOPLE'S NATURAL RIGHT TO A SHARE IN THE LEGISLATURE;

Which is the

FUNDAMENTAL PRINCIPLE

OF THE

BRITISH CONSTITUTION OF STATE.

By GRANVILLE SHARP.

"Qui non libere veritatem pronunciat, prodi-
"tor eſt veritatis." 4 Inſt. Epil.

LONDON:
Printed for B. WHITE, at HORACE's-HEAD,
in FLEET-STREET.
M.DCC.LXXIV.

PREFACE.

THE following "Declaration "of the People's natural Right "to a Share in the Legiſlature" is founded on Principles, which are certainly unqueſtionable, and cannot eaſily be controverted; but I was not aware, I acknowledge, (1) when I ſent the ſame to the Preſs, that there had ever been any Controverſy before the 6th of King George I. concerning the Freedom of our fellow-ſubjects in *Ireland*, or that any Engliſhman, acquainted with the principles of our excellent Conſtitution of State, had ever, before that time, preſumed to advance any doctrine which might tend to deprive our Iriſh Brethren

a of

(1) I freely acknowledge my deficiency in *hiſtorical* as well as moſt other branches of Learning, which require much reading and leiſure to be obtained; but though this affords an argument againſt *my own perſonal credit and abilities, in general*, as a writer, yet it does not at all affect any particular point, which, in my ſeveral tracts, I have laboured to maintain; for, upon theſe, a candid Reader will determine according to the evidence produced, and not by the general character or *demerit* of the Author in other reſpects.

of their *natural Freedom*, and of the inestimable benefits of that happy legal Constitution, which British Subjects in general are commonly supposed to inherit by *Birth-right!*

If I had not esteemed this point *incontrovertible*, when I wrote the said *Declaration*, I should not have quoted the Union between *Great Britain* and *Ireland* as an example of "*the true constitu-*"*tional* mode of *connecting British Do-*"*minions* that are otherwise *separated by* "*nature*." But having done this, and having also given several copies of the Declaration to my friends which cannot now be recalled, I have thereby brought upon myself the necessity of maintaining the propriety of the said example, which might as easily have been avoided, had I been aware of any such controversy; because the general principles, on which my arguments are founded, would have been amply sufficient (I apprehend) to prove the truth of my *Declaration*, even though *Examples* and *Custom* had been against it; for the Common Law of *England* teaches us, that examples and precedents are not to be followed if they are *unreasonable*, or inconsistent with

legal

legal and *constitutional* Principles (2); though, on the other hand, they are to be esteemed of very great weight and authority in Law, when there are *no just exceptions* against them (3). And of this latter kind is the Example which I have quoted to illustrate my Declaration: for, though many great and respectable Writers have made *exceptions* to the constitutional Freedom of *Ireland*, which I had supposed to be unquestionable, yet, after the most careful examination of their opinions, and the *reasons* given for the same, (in which the proofs ought to consist,) I am now fully convinced that there are *no just exceptions* against that example; and, consequently, I am bound in justice to my fellow-subjects in *Ireland* not to give it up; because the

 "*necessity*"

(2) This is clearly proved by a variety of unquestionable maxims;

"Judicandum est *Legibus*, *non Exemplis*."

"Malus usus abolendus est."

"In consuetudinibus non diuturnitas temporis, sed "*soliditas rationis*, consideranda est."

"Multitudo *errantium* non parit *errori* patroci-"nium."

(3) —— et quia consuetudines illæ *nec contra legem* "*divinam nec contra rationem* in aliquo existunt, et "pro bono communi totius Regni ex earum diurni-"tate censentur, fore necessariæ, *vim Legis retinent*," &c. Doct. et Stud. c. 7.

" *necessity*" (beforementioned) " of main-" taining the *propriety of the example*," cited in my Declaration, arises not from any obstinate partiality to my own assertion, (which I confess was, at first, too hastily and unadvisedly made,) but from a firm persuasion, after a most cautious enquiry into the real state of the controversy, that the advocates for the Liberties of *Ireland* have Truth and Reason on their side, which, (I hope) the 2d Part, now added to my Declaration, will sufficiently testify.

It is necessary also for me to guard against another objection which might perhaps hereafter have been started against the following *Declaration*.

I have quoted therein a maxim of the English Constitution, as a principle of *natural equity*, which had previously been denied that rank by one of the most eminent civilians of his time; and therefore, to avoid the influence of so great an authority against my Argument, I think it prudent, in this Preface, to examine the grounds of his objections, that my Readers may have sufficient evidence before them to distinguish where the truth lies; for it is certainly necessary for me to to eſtabliſh the firſt *principles* on which I have proceeded, before I can expect to have any attention paid to the Arguments which I have built upon them.

The maxim which I wiſh to maintain is as follows, *viz.* that " Law, to bind " all, muſt be aſſented to by all (4)." This maxim I have quoted in the following Declaration as a principle of *natural Equity*; though, it ſeems, the learned Civilian, Baron Puffendorf, has expreſſly refuſed to rank it with the *Laws of Nature:* He, or (rather I ſhould ſay) his Tranſlator, calls (5) it only *a notion.*

" We cannot here but obſerve," (ſays he,) " that the *Notion,* maintained by " ſome authors, *That the Conſent of the* " *People is requiſite to make Laws oblige* " *the Subject in Conſcience,* is neither " true *in the Laws of Nature,* nor in the " civil Laws of monarchical or of ariſto- " cratical Rulers; nor indeed at all, un- " leſs it be underſtood of implicit con- " ſent; as a man, by agreeing to the " Sovereignty

(4) Principia Leg. et Æquit. p. 56. to which is added, by way of illuſtration, " Canons therefore bind " not the Laity."

(5) The Edition which I have followed is only an Engliſh tranſlation printed at Oxford in 1710.

"Sovereignty of another, is at the ſame "time, ſuppoſed to have agreed to all "the future Acts of that Sovereignty(6)." (He has nevertheleſs thought proper to add an obſervation which makes ſtrongly againſt his own argument.) "Though it would really be very uſeful," (ſays he,) "and contribute much to engaging the "Subjects in a *voluntary Obedience*, if "the Laws could be made *with their* "*Conſent* and Approbation; eſpecially "ſuch as are to paſs into their Lives and "Manners."

Now it would be impoſſible (I apprehend) to find ſo juſt a reaſon in favour of the former part of the learned Baron's aſſertion, as he himſelf has here given *directly againſt it*; and yet he is frequently harping upon the ſame harſh ſtring of abſolute implicit obedience; which inconſiſtency cannot eaſily be accounted for, unleſs it be attributed to *the prejudice of his education* as a ſtudent in *the Imperial or Civil Law*. For though the Civil Law contains many excellent maxims highly worthy of our eſteem, moſt of which have been adopted by our ancient

(6) Law of Nature and Nations, Book 1. c. 6. p. 55.

cient English writers of the Common Law of this Kingdom (7); yet it includes some heterogeneous positions (that have been forced upon it by the overbearing influence and corrupt practices of unlimited Imperial Courts) which are highly unreasonable and contradictory to the general equity of its other principles. A position of this kind, too implicitly received as Law, seems to be the groundwork of the learned Baron's difficulty: I mean that *unreasonable* and dangerous position of the Civil Law, which attributes to the Prince's *Will and Pleasure* the *Force* of Law (8). I do not find, indeed,

(7) "What use our ancestors have made of the civil "Law will readily appear to any one, that will take "the trouble to compare the several works, which com- "pose that voluminous body, with some of the most "ancient English Lawyers, as Glanvil, Bracton, "and others; who have adhered very closely to the "rules and method of Justinian; have transcribed his "Laws in their own proper language, and some- "times entire titles, as familiarly as if they were the "original Laws of England." Dr. Bever's Discourse on the Study of Juris-prudence and the Civil Law, p. 17.

(8) "Quod Principi placuit (juxta Leges Civiles) "Legis habet vigorem." Fortescue de Laud. Leg. Ang. c. 35. p. 83.

In this same chapter the learned Chancellor Fortescue recites many dreadful effects of this abominable principle

deed, that he has literally cited the corrupt maxims, but he has manifestly laid down

principle in the Government and Police of *France*. viz. the pernicious and dangerous Policy of maintaining a *standing army*; for which the people were compelled to provide quarters and provisions, in all the great towns and villages.

Also the abominable oppression of the Salt Tax, whereby the poor were compelled to purchase of the King a certain quantity of *Salt* (whether they chose to have it or not) at an excessive price; by which, together with the assessments *to pay the troops*, and various other tallage rateable at the *King's pleasure*, the common people were reduced to extreme penury, and want of every comfort in life. And, with respect to persons of higher rank, if any Nobleman or Gentleman was accused of a crime, even by his enemies, he was liable to be dragged to a *private examination*, by the intermediation of messengers in the King's chamber, or elsewhere, in a private place, without seeing his accusers (himself alone being seen); and when the King (or perhaps his Minister) has *been pleased* to judge him guilty, the poor *passive Subject* is popped into a sack, and in the night time cast into the river by the Marshal's servants. Howsoever incredible such abominable injustice may appear to Englishmen, yet the worthy Chancellor, who wrote this account for the instruction of Edward Prince of Wales (the son of King Henry VI.) when in France, appeals to the young Prince's *own knowledge* of the notoriety of such facts: "You have heard," (says he) "that more "men (by much) have died in this manner than by "the ordinary course of justice; yet nevertheless" (says he ironically) "*whatsoever hath pleased the King* "*(according to the Civil Law) has the force of Law.* "And while you have been in France, and in the "neighbourhood of that Kingdom," (continues the Chancellor

down the same principle (though in different words) towards the beginning of

Chancellor to the young Prince,) "you have heard of "other *enormities* like to these, and some even worse "than these—*detestably* and *damnably perpetrated*, no "otherwise than under the colour (or pretence) of "*that Law*, *viz.* Quod Principi placuit (juxta Leges "Civiles) legis habet vigorem." "Etiam et alia *enor-"mia*," (says he) "hiis similia, ac quædam *hiis deteriora*, "dum in Francia et prope regnum illud conversatus es, "audisti non alio, quam *legis illius colore* DETESTABILI-"TUR DAMNABILITERQUE PERPETRATA, quæ hic "inserere, nostrum nimium dialogum protelaret," *&c.* Whether or not *this particular mode* of dispatching the French King's Subjects is yet in use, I know not; but of this we are well assured, that *private executions of persons unknown* are still practised there, which in effect are *equally dangerous*, and cannot be considered in any other light than that of so many *wilful Murders*, for which the Kings of France, and all those men whom they have intrusted with the administration of Justice, are most certainly accountable, and must one day answer in their own private persons *as individuals*, besides the enormous guilt which lies heavy upon that whole people as a *nation*, for *passively* permitting such notorious and crying *iniquity* to be practised among them under the borrowed *name* of *Law*: And it is not only *the dispatching of men* (to put them out of the way of opposition to Government) that is intended by these *midnight executions*, but also, in some cases, to satisfy a base malicious revenge by torturing the helpless victim with the cruel death of *breaking on the wheel*; for, as both the *name* and *crime* of the *sufferer is concealed*, (or perhaps a wrong name given out to prevent pity,) it cannot be said that such cruelty is used by way *of example* to deter bad men from commiting treason, or other particular crimes; so that

the same chapter, where he is defining the difference between *Law* and some other

such *private executions* can be attributed to nothing but a DIABOLICAL DEPRAVITY in the minds of those who order them.

It also appears that one use of a *standing Army*, in that unhappy Kingdom, is to guard the avenues of streets to prevent the people from discovering the *actors* as well as *sufferers* at such horrid *masked tragedies* as I have mentioned; and therefore I cannot help remarking the extreme absurdity of that (otherwise) sensible and shrewd people in boasting of their *national military Honour*, when even large bodies of their best-disciplined troops, who are *Frenchmen* also by birth, and have the means in their own hands to render justice and restore liberty to their *much-injured countrymen*, can yet tamely yield themselves so far to the *absolute Will* of any man or men on earth, as to become *silent accomplices* (like the detestable Turkish *Mutes* of old) to the horrid crime of *wilful Murder*, (for such are the *secret executions* of France,) and professed *Tools* for perpetrating the most abandoned wickedness! To such a disgraceful and *slavish* pitch of *passive obedience* is that once-spirited nation now reduced, that they seem to give up all pretensions to that *fundamental Right of human Nature*, which alone distinguishes *men* from *brutes!* I mean the indispensible *Right of judging for themselves*, and of yielding obedience to the impulse of *Conscience*, according to that natural knowledge of *good and evil* which is implanted in *all men*, (*French soldiers* as well as others,) and of which they must one day render a strict account in a separate *disbanded* state, as *individuals*, (which I have before remarked,) *stript of their arms and regimentals!*

Shall we, then, adopt the *Laws of France?* "*quod* "*principi placuit?*" &c. It is not impossible that such a measure may sometime or other be proposed by an inconsiderate Minister, and that a Parliament (through the

other things, which seem to bear relation to it; as *Counsel*, which requires *reasons* to produce an *obligation*, &c.

"But *Law*," (says he,) "though it "ought not to want its *reasons*, yet these "*reasons* are not the cause why obe-"dience is paid to it, *but the power of* "*the Exactor*; who, when he has sig-"nified his *pleasure*, lays an *obligation* "on the *Subjects* to act in conformity to "his decree, though perhaps they do "not so well apprehend the *reasons* of "the injunction," *&c.* and, after citing a similar passage from Mr. Hobbs, he adds;

 "For

the *unequal Representation of the* People, the *want of frequent elections*, and other defects in the constitution, *&c.*) may hereafter be led to yield their consent to it; but, even if ever that should be the case, I shall still entertain hopes, from the general disposition of our *British* Troops, (notwithstanding the alarming effects of *standing Armies* in all other Nations,) that they will never become so detestably base and degenerate as to permit their country to groan under any such iniquitous Oppressions as are practised in *France*! Nevertheless, should *they also* become such *slavish Tools of Despotism*, as to assist in enforcing any such unconstitutional measures, let them know, for a certainty, that, as soon as the *national Spirit of Freedom* (of which they at present participate) is, by their means, unhappily suppressed, even they themselves must necessarily degenerate with their countrymen, and will be no more able to stand before their enemies, than the other wretched troops whom they have so often driven before them!

" For no man can ſay, *ſic volo, ſic ju-*
" *beo*; ſo I will, and ſo I command;
" unleſs,

" —— Stet pro *Ratione voluntas.*"
" His *Will* is his *Reaſon.*"

" We obey Laws, therefore," (ſays he,) " not principally upon account of the " matter of them, but upon account of " *the Legiſlator's Will* (9)."

Thus the learned Civilian ſeems to conſider *the Will and Pleaſure* of a Sovereign as the life and ſpirit of Laws; which *notion* is highly *unreaſonable* in every caſe but one, *viz.* when we are ſpeaking of the Laws of that Sovereign alone, whoſe *Will* is the fountain of *Reaſon*, and whoſe *Pleaſure* (by our own natural *Reaſon* we are convinced) is infinite *goodneſs*, *juſtice*, and *mercy*, towards all thoſe to whom he has ſignified his commands; becauſe we cannot ſeparate the *idea* of infallible *Reaſon*, *Wiſdom*, and eternal *Juſtice*, from any command of divine authority.

And yet this application of the Baron's doctrine, even to the *ſupreme* Law, is not conformable throughout to what I underſtand

(9) Book 1, chap. 6. §. 1.

understand in this place of the Baron's idea of *Law*; for he assigns no other "cause why obedience is paid to it, but "the *power* of *the Exactor*;" whereas God's Laws have many other apparent *causes* of *obligation*, of which I have already mentioned the due sense we *naturally* entertain of the infinite *Wisdom* and *Truth* (as well as *the Power*) of the Divine Author, who is so far from being *an Exactor* of *Laws*, that the revelation of his will for the good government of mankind has generally been addressed to the *Senses* and *Reason* of Men, that their *Covenant* with God might be founded on *free Consent*, the highest and most obligatory *Cause of Obedience*.

Now, as the Laws of God are thus tendered to us under the equitable form of a *reciprocal Covenant*, thereby binding even himself (the supreme Lord and Creator of all things) to us, his poor mortal subjects, under *conditional Promises* which cannot fail on his part! how much more ought all mere *worldly* Governors to be restrained and limited by equitable *Covenants* of *mutual obligation* between them and their Subjects, since their *equality* in nature gives the

the latter an undoubted Right to inſiſt on this, the only ſafe mode of worldly Government?

The conſideration of this point leads me to one of the principal Grounds of Baron Puffendorf's Miſtake, beforementioned.

He does not ſeem to have been aware, that, in all ſocieties of men governed by *Laws*, ſome ſort of *general Covenant* muſt be underſtood to ſubſiſt between the ſeveral *Sovereigns* and their *Subjects* reſpectively: and, though ſuch *Covenants* are not always *expreſſed*, yet, moſt certainly, they are always *implied*; becauſe we muſt neceſſarily preſume, that *the Good of the People* is the original intention and principal end of all *legal* human Governments, ſince *all Men are naturally equals*, and *a Man* who ſubmits himſelf to the Sovereignty or Government of another, that he may enjoy the benefit and protection of ſociety, does not, on that account, ceaſe to be *a Man*; neither can the temporal Sovereign himſelf be releaſed from the *natural* Tyes of *that Relation*: for, whenever he forgets that he himſelf is *a Man*, (of the ſame fallible underſtanding and natural infirmities with

with his Subjects, who are his *equals* both on their *entrance* and at their *exeunt* from the Stage of Life,) he immediately loses the best Rule for his Conduct as *a Prince*, and necessarily degenerates into *brutality*; so that, in such cases, to suppose that THE WILL *of the Prince* is to be allowed *the force of Law* is the highest absurdity! Nay, even the Baron himself has elsewhere declared, that "the word MAN, is thought to carry "somewhat of *Dignity* in its sound; and "we commonly" (says he) "make use "of this as the last and the most prevailing argument against a rude insulter, "*I am not a Beast, a Dog, but I am* A "MAN *as well as yourself*. Since then "*human* nature agrees *equally* to all persons, and since no one can live a sociable life with another, who does not "own and respect him as *a Man*; it follows, as a command of the Law of "Nature, *that* EVERY MAN *esteem and* "*treat* ANOTHER as one who is naturally HIS EQUAL, or who is A MAN as "well as he." (Book 3, c. 2. p. 178.) It would therefore be unreasonable to conceive, that any society of MEN should voluntarily submit themselves to a temporal

ral Sovereign, without ſuppoſing, at the ſame time, ſome *reciprocal obligation* or *duty* to ſubſiſt between them; which is nothing elſe but the *implication* of a mutual *Covenant:* and, indeed, the formalities of every Coronation ſufficiently indicate and warrant ſuch an *implication*; and the infringements made by Monarchs on ſuch *implied Covenants* have, in all ages, been occaſionally puniſhed by the expulſion and deſtruction of the Tyrants themſelves, of which moſt nations have, at ſome time or other, afforded an example.

Nevertheleſs, the learned Baron ſeems to have neglected theſe neceſſary conſiderations; for he aſſerts, that the diſtinction between a *Compact* or *Covenant*, and a *Law*, is obvious. "For a *Com-* "*pact*" (ſays he) "is a *Promiſe*, but a "*Law* is a *Command.* In Compacts the "form of ſpeaking is *I will* do ſo and "ſo; but in Law the form runs, *do thou* "*ſo*, after an imperative manner." Book 1. c. 6. §. 2. p. 47.

He had before been ſpeaking of democratical Governments, and had remarked, not only that the ancients "frequently "apply to Laws the name of *common* "*Agreements*," but alſo, that "the Laws" (among

(among the Grecians) "were made upon "the proposal of the Magistrate, with "the Knowledge, and *by the Command* "*of the People*, and so" (as it were) "in the way of *bargain or stipulation*," (says he,) "they gave them the name of "*Covenants* and *Agreements* beforemen-"tioned:" and yet he will not allow (notwithstanding such authority) that they are properly stiled "*Covenants*," having puzzled himself with the difference between a national *Covenant* and a *Covenant* of individuals; "for, in this last "case," (says he,) "a person that *dissents* "*is not bound*, and the party cannot pro-"ceed without him; whereas, in the for-"mer *case*, even the *dissenting Party* is "tied and obliged by the plurality of "votes." Now the learned Baron has not been aware that this very reason, which he himself has assigned, confirms the propriety of that ancient custom which he condemns, (*viz.* the applying the name of *Covenants* and *Agreements* to *Laws*,) for, he allows, that "the *dissent-*"*ing Party* is tied and obliged by *the plu-*"*rality of votes*," and therefore, even a whole nation, in that case, may be said to act as *an individual*; because, "*that to*

" *which the greater number give consent*" (as he himself remarks in the preceding paragraph) " *is taken* for the *Will and De-* " *cree of all*;" so that, by this means, a *whole Nation* is as capable of making a *Covenant* or *Compact* as an *Individual*; and I will only add, to what the Baron has allowed about the *binding* of *those who dissent*, that they are bound *only so far* as the imposed *Obligation* is consistent with their *superior Covenant* and duty to God, which is always to be *implied*: for even the SOVEREIGN of *the World*, THE KING OF KINGS, who alone can be said to have an *absolute Right* to govern his creature man *without a free Covenant*, (if he had been pleased so to do,) has nevertheless condescended to include all his positive *Laws* in two express *legal Covenants*, the *old* and the *new*, both of which have been from time to time confirmed and fulfilled, and still respectively subsist to this day in all points, wherein the former is not superseded, and fulfilled by the latter. It therefore ill becomes this learned Civilian to separate the idea of a *Compact* or *Covenant from Law*; and more especially when he endeavours thereby to establish " *the Power of the* " *Exactor*,"

" *Exactor*," the capricious *Will* of mere temporal fallible Sovereigns, which he supposes to be *Law*, independent of all *Compacts* or *Covenants* expressed or implied!

Thus I hope I have traced, to the very foundation, the Baron's error in denying the principle or maxim beforementioned, (concerning the necessity of popular *assent* in Legislation,) for, if he had not attempted to separate the idea of a *Covenant* from *Law*, he could not have overlooked the absolute *illegality* of those pretended Laws which are ordained only by the *Will* and " *Power of the Exac-" tor!*" because the meanest professor of the English common Law would have told him, that every submission, *promise*, or *agreement*, that is *extorted* by *fear* and *compulsion*, is (according to the *Law of Nature)* totally *null and void in itself*; and he himself is sufficiently sensible of this in another place (10). And, even if an

(10) " Those *promises* then, or *pacts*, we take to be " *invalid*, which a man is *compelled* to engage in, by " the *unjust force* of the party to whom they are made; " for since he, who *extorts* any thing from another by " using unjust terrours, is *by the Law of Nature* bound " to restore it, and must consequently make good " what

an oath ſhould be obtained to confirm the unjuſt " *Power of the Exactor*," it will not increaſe his Right; for the Baron's own doctrine (again in another part of his book) affords a ſufficient anſwer to annul every pretence of *Obligation* on account of " *oaths extorted by un-*" *juſt Fear* (11)."

Thus the maxim concerning *the neceſſity of Aſſent*, for which I contend, is ſufficiently proved to be a *Law of Nature* even by the learned Baron's own arguments, and I deſire no better.

In conſequence of the Baron's general miſconception (12), concerning the neceſſity

" what the other perſon loſes by ſuch forced bargain, " the neceſſity of *Reparation*, in the party who offered " the violence, *takes off* ALL OBLIGATION *to payment* " *in the party who ſuffered it*, &c." Book 3. c. 6. §. 11. p. 225.

(11) " But what are we to think of *oaths* extorted " by *unjuſt Fear?* Surely the Perſon who, by means of " this *Fear*, procured a promiſe *upon oath*, is no leſs " obliged to *releaſe the promiſe*, thus violently obtained, " than *if no oath had been* added to confirm it. There- " fore there appears no reaſon, why *Compenſation* ſhould " not be admitted in this caſe, in oppoſition to *the* " *Claim* of the *injurious Party*; according to the rules " laid down by us" (ſays he) " when we treated of " the general ſubject of *Fear*." Book 4. c. 2. §. 8. p. 272.

(12) I have ſpent the more time in warning my Readers againſt the Errors of this celebrated Civilian, becauſe

ceſſity of *agreement* to make Laws valid, he has aſſerted alſo, "that neither the "*divine poſitive Laws*, nor the *Laws of* "*Nature*, had their riſe from the *agree-* "*ment of men*," &c. Book 1. c. 6. §. 2. p. 47.

Now his obſervation is certainly *true* as far as it relates to the *riſe* or *origin* of ſuch Laws; for the Laws, being *divine*, muſt neceſſarily have "*had their riſe*" from God; but yet this does not ſet aſide "*the*

cauſe the ſtudying of his Works (I am informed) is at this time conſidered as a material part of Education in our Univerſities; ſo that *the riſing Generation* of the very beſt Families in this Kingdom are liable to imbibe (as it were with the Milk of Inſtruction) theſe poiſonous Doctrines, which thereby become fixed and engrafted in their tender minds as a *foundation* for their *future political Principles!*

Thus a moſt dangerous ſource of unconſtitutional notions has been opened, and ſeems already to have flowed throughout the Kingdom; ſo that we need not wonder at the *modern partiality* for increaſing the number as well as the powers of *Courts of Admiralty*, and other ſeminaries of the *Civil Law*, though the very exiſtence of *Britiſh Liberty* depends on duly reſtraining and limiting the *Civil Law Courts* within thoſe bounds of juriſdiction which have been allowed them by the ancient Conſtitution of this Kingdom: And therefore I hope my Readers will excuſe my having exceeded the uſual form of publications, in making *ſo long* a Preface to *ſo ſhort* a Work, ſince it was abſolutely neceſſary to guard againſt theſe dangerous and inveterate errors of the *Civil Law*, before I could ſafely proceed to my Declaration in favour of *popular Aſſent*.

" *the agreement of men*," by which they have been ratified and confirmed in all ages. The Baron ſeems to have overlooked the information we have received from Scripture, that men inherit a *divine attribute* from their parents, I mean that *knowledge of good and evil* which they took upon themſelves contrary to the *expreſs command of God*, and thereby unhappily entailed Sin and Death on all their poſterity; for that *divine knowledge* neceſſarily engages and includes our *agreement* or *aſſent* to the " *the Laws of Nature*," whether we obey them or not, and thereby renders us *anſwerable* for our imperfect conduct in this world, and conſequently *guilty before God!* And from hence ariſes the neceſſity of a redemption to relieve mankind from that unhappy effect of the *Original Sin*; for, as "*the ſtrength of " Sin is the Law*," (13) ſo the guilt of every criminal action is *with juſtice imputed* to us, becauſe we have *wilfully* offended againſt this *natural light* or *Law in our Hearts*, by which we ought to have known how *to refuſe the* EVIL *and choose the* GOOD.

This

(13) " The ſting of Death is Sin; and the *ſtrength of " Sin is the Law*." 1 Cor. xv. 56.

This knowledge of *Good and Evil* was discovered, even by the Gentiles, *to be a divine attribute* (14), though they were unacquainted, probably, with the occasion of its being engrafted in human nature. It must therefore appear, that the *agreement* or *assent* of mankind to the moral and eternal Laws of God (which the Baron and other Civilians commonly call "the *Laws of Nature*") may very fairly be presumed and admitted as a natural effect of the human understanding, whenever any of the said Laws are mentioned; for, all persons, who have any reflection, must

(14) Cicero calls this natural knowledge of Good and Evil, *Law*. "Lex" (says he in his first Book De Legibus) "est *ratio summa*, insita *in natura*, quæ *jubet* ea quæ facienda sunt, *prohibetque* contraria; *eadem ratio* cum est in hominis mente confirmata et confecta *Lex* est." And in his third Book De Officiis, where he is speaking again of natural Reason, he calls it *a Divine Law*.—"Ipsa naturæ ratio, quæ est *Lex divina* et humana:"——And elsewhere he more particularly declares it to be a *Divine Attribute*.—"Recta, et *a numine Deorum* tracta *ratio*." And he mentions this *attribute* again in his second Book "*De Natura Deorum*," where he speaks of *prudence*, or "the *choice of Good* and *rejection of Evil*," as a universal Law, *common to God and man*. "Sequitur ut *eadem* sit in *his* (Diis) quæ in *genere humano*, *ratio*, *eadem veritas* utrobique sit, *eademque Lex*; quæ est *recti præceptio pravique depulsio*. Ex quo intelligitur, *prudentiam* quoque, et *mentem a Diis* ad homines, pervenisse," *&c*.

muſt be ſenſible that we ſtand ſelf-condemned by *Conſcience* (which is only another name for " *the knowledge of Good " and Evil*") whenever we offend againſt *the moral Laws* of God, by which our *Agreement* and *Aſſent* to the juſtice of them are ſufficiently *implied* and acknowledged (15): And, with reſpect to what the Baron has likewiſe inſinuated concerning the want of *human agreement* to the " *divine poſitive Laws*," the direct contrary thereto is clearly demonſtrated (as I have before hinted) by the remarkable examples of two inconteſtible legal *Covenants* between *God and Man*, the Old and New Teſtaments, thoſe two original written *Charters or Grants* of PERFECT LIBERTY; the one containing the *Promiſes*, and the other, the *Accompliſhment* of our *glorious Freedom*; which we are bound to maintain and defend to the laſt moment of our lives!

The mention that has already been made of theſe two unqueſtionable monuments of the *free State and Condition*, to which the Almighty has been pleaſed to invite

(15) I have traced this ſubject more at large in a ſeparate Tract on " the *Law of Nature and Principles of Action in* MAN," intended alſo for the Preſs.

invite his creature Man, might perhaps be ſufficient for my preſent purpoſe, without deſcending to farther particulars; but yet, as I received extraordinary ſatisfaction myſelf in tracing minutely the manner in which the ſaid Covenants have been tendered and ratified, I am inclined to ſuppoſe that many of my Readers will reap the ſame ſatisfaction by peruſing ſome examples of it, becauſe they demonſtrate the *real dignity* and *natural Rights* of MAN, far beyond any thing that I could poſſibly have conceived before I made the ſaid Examination with this particular view to the *Freedom* of Man; and as I have too much reaſon to apprehend, that many of my countrymen have overlooked or neglected theſe *ſtriking Inſtances*, which relate to the preſent ſubject, the *Right of Aſſent*; I propoſe to add (ſometime hereafter, as ſoon as I can poſſibly find leiſure to reviſe it for the preſs) a *third Part* alſo to this "Declaration "of the People's natural Right to a Share "in the Legiſlature;" which 3*d Part* (being founded on ſome remarkable examples in Scripture, concerning the gracious and moſt liberal mode whereby the *revealed Laws, even of God himſelf*, have been

 tendered

tendered (from time to time) to the confideration and acceptance of mankind) proves by comparative demonftration, that the MAXIMS OF THE FOREIGN CIVILIANS, whereby they fet up the mere WILL of fallible earthly Princes as LAW, (viz. *Quod Principi placuit habet vigorem Legis.—Stet pro ratione voluntas. &c.* fubftituting WILL for REASON,) are IMPIOUS AND UNJUST; fince even the ALMIGHTY SOVEREIGN OF THE UNIVERSE, to whofe WILL alone fuch deference is *juftly due*, hath not fo dealt with his creature Man, enforcing his *Will* for his *Reafon*; but, on the contrary, hath mercifully condefcended to convince us (his frail mortal fubjects) that REASON is his WILL, and that he hath *limited* (if I may be allowed fuch an expreffion) even his own *infinite Power* by the eternal rules of Juftice and Righteoufnefs, which, (our own *natural Reafon* teaches us,) can never fail! and therefore, as true *Freedom* confifts in the *certainty* of known Laws, fo the moft *perfect Liberty* muft neceffarily fubfift under the Government of the *Almighty*; who has appealed by his prophets from time to time, in the moft affecting manner,

ner, to the *reaſon* and *ſenſes* of mankind, that his Laws might be confirmed by a *voluntary popular Aſſent*, the only true foundation of all valid *Compacts*; and that the ſaid Laws have accordingly been ſolemnly *ratified*, and voluntarily accepted by the people, in two *mutual Compacts*, or *Covenants*, (commonly called the Old and New Teſtaments,) whereby not only the People are bound *on their part*, but even the ETERNAL KING HIMSELF is *conditionally* bound alſo *on his part* to the performance of the *moſt glorious Promiſes!* (16)

And

(16) The promiſes of God are made to all mankind (without exception) who receive and keep his *Covenant*; ſo that every true believer, be his rank in life ever ſo mean, is undoubtedly capable of becoming "*an a-*" *dopted Son* of God *;"—" A temple of God," by the inward *dwelling* of his Holy Spirit †: —" An heir of " ſalvation ‡;"—" *a joint heir with Chriſt* ||;" and all

* —— "That we might receive *the adoption of ſons*," (ſaid the Apoſtle to the Galatians;) " and, becauſe *ye are ſons*, God hath ſent " forth the Spirit of *his Son* into your hearts, crying *Abba, Father!*" Gal. iv. 5. 6.

† —— " Know ye not that ye are the temple of God, and that " the Spirit of God *dwelleth* in you? If any man defile the temple of " God, *him ſhall God deſtroy*: for *the Temple of God* is holy, which " temple *ye are*." 1 Cor. iii. 16. 17. See alſo 2 Cor. vi. 16.

‡ —— " That the Gentiles ſhould be *fellow-heirs*, and of the " ſame body, and partakers of his promiſe in Chriſt by the Goſpel." Eph. iii. 6.

|| —— " If children, then heirs; heirs of God, and JOINT " HEIRS WITH CHRIST." Romans viii. 17.

And he hath accordingly inſtituted by his Son (the *eternal Word*, in whom "*dwelleth all the fulneſs of the* GOD-"HEAD *bodily*," Col. ii. 9.) not only a *Form* for the admiſſion of new Members or *Parties* to his free COVENANT, but alſo ordained a ſolemn rite for the *renewal and acknowledgement* of the ſaid COVENANT from time to time at *his holy Table*, from which the Subjects of his Kingdom cannot ſafely abſtain without ſeeming to deny that *allegiance* and *homage* which they indiſpenſibly owe to their eternal Sovereign!

I had

all ſuch ſhall "COME WITH HIM TO JUDGE THE "WORLD §!" Now as the *eternal* dignity, to which *human* nature is invited, is ſo *great* and *glorious*, can we ſuppoſe that God has not ſome regard alſo for the *temporal* Rights of his highly-favoured creature, Man? How, then, can any particular Man, or body of Men, preſume to ſet up their own WILL for LAW, and thereby deprive their *Brethren* of that *Right*, which, of all others, is moſt eſſential to *reaſonable* beings, I mean the *Right* of *Aſſent*? Let thoſe men, who thus inconſiderately venture to affront the *dignity of mankind*, by withholding from them their *temporal* Rights, (*viz. Choice, Freewill*, and the due exerciſe of that *Reaſon* which God has given them,) beware leſt they themſelves ſhould thereby forfeit their own eternal privileges!—"Know "ye not that *we ſhall judge Angels?—how much more "things that pertain to this Life?* 1 Cor. vi. 3.

§ —— For "the *ſaints ſhall judge the world*." 1 Cor. vi. 2.

I had intended alſo to have added to this Declaration a little Tract on "*the* "*Law Eternal*, which limits Legiſla-" ture, and forms the Baſis of the Subjects "Rights;" but the ſame Reaſon, which obliged me to poſtpone the *Third Part* of the Declaration already mentioned, obliges me to defer this alſo for the preſent: Nevertheleſs, as my Declaration is founded on many of the *principles* and *maxims* of that ſame "*eternal Law*," I ſhall beg leave to add to this Preface a ſhort quotation from the ſaid Tract, concerning the weight, uſe, and manner, of applying the *maxims*, or rules, of *eternal Reaſon*: which is the more neceſſary at this time, becauſe I find there are great numbers of people who are ſo ill informed of theſe matters as to talk of "the "*omnipotence* of *Parliament*," as if they conceived, that every thing whatſoever, that is ordained by Parliament, muſt be *Law*, whether it be *good* or *evil*, right or wrong!—A moſt pernicious and baneful Doctrine this!—A kind of *Popery in Politics*, (if I may uſe ſuch an expreſſion,) which is dangerous to the *eternal* as well as *temporal* happineſs of mankind!

'The

'The welfare and happineſs of So-
'ciety, indeed, require, that every indivi-
'dual, from the higheſt to the loweſt,
'ſhould have ſome *general idea of Law*;
'but more particularly is this requiſite in
'*England*, where the *People* enjoy (as
'the moſt valuable Heritage derived from
'their anceſtors) the natural and moſt
'equitable *Right* of forming a part of
'the *legiſlative Power*.

'*Law* is indeed a very comprehenſive
'Term, which includes ſuch a prodi-
'gious fund of abſtruſe learning, that a
'*particular and accurate knowledge of it*
'is ſcarcely to be acquired with the ut-
'moſt aſſiduity and labour even of a man's
'whole life; and yet a *general* idea of
'*Law* (I mean that which is *immutable*
'and *eternal*, and which forms the
'*ground* and *baſis* of all other *Laws*)
'may nevertheleſs be very eaſily *in-*
'*culcated* and as eaſily *retained*; becauſe
'the great out-lines, or rather *the Ele-*
'*ments and firſt Principles, of the* LAW
'conſiſt of *the moſt obvious and ſelf-evident*
'*concluſions* of REASON, which are
'*implanted in our very* NATURE; ſince
'we inherit from our firſt Parents the
'*Knowledge*

'*Knowledge of Good and Evil* (17),' (beforementioned) 'by which, every 'Man who is not an ideot, or madman, '(that is, *every Man of* COMMON SENSE,) 'is *naturally* enabled to receive, diſcern, 'and approve, *the firſt Elements* or 'leading principles of LAW and REA-'SON, when fairly propoſed to him in 'his

(17) "*Good and Evil* are not matters of Law or of "Logic. They are the moſt, if not the only, eſſential "circumſtances of the world. They are what every "thing elſe refers to. They ſtamp an eternal mark "and difference on all things, which even imagina-"tion cannot cancel or eraſe. The enjoyment of the "*one*, and the avoiding of the *other*, is the very end of "our being, and likewiſe of all the beings which do "or which even can be ſuppoſed to exiſt, and which have "a ſenſe and perception of them. Whatever therefore "relates *to the general* GOOD *and* EVIL *of a People* is of a "*public nature*. It is that circumſtance which makes it "ſo. The terms are as good as ſynonimous. Whatever "concerns, on the contrary, only this or that indi-"vidual, is of a private nature. It is confined to "his or their *happineſs* or *welfare*; to his or their "*good* and *evil*. There is again the true and unerring "criterion. Theſe things ſeem clear to the greateſt de-"gree of intuitive certainty. It is ſtrange to be forced "to reaſon about them!" Conſiderations on the Meaſures carrying on with reſpect to the Britiſh Colonies in North America. 2d Edit. p. 156, 157.

The "Conſiderations" indeed of this ſenſible Author, in every other part of his work, highly merit the moſt ſerious attention of all thoſe perſons (of what party ſoever) who deſire real information and good council concerning the preſent diſputes with our Brethren in *America*.

'his own language; and these same 'Elements and their *supreme* incontrovertible authority being once known and 'acknowledged, it is very easy, in general, for any Man of *Common Sense* to 'discern, by comparison, what is contrary 'and repugnant thereto; for THE LAW 'is compared to a RULE, or RIGHT 'LINE,—"*Lex est Linea Recti*,"—by 'which every thing that is *oblique*, *crooked*, '*transverse*, or different from that RIGHT 'LINE is easily known to the meanest 'capacity; and therefore, *in the Law*, "the RIGHT LINE *is always to be* "PREFERRED," "*Linea recta semper* "*præfertur transversali*." Co. Lib. 10. b. 'And from hence it arises, that 'the adjectives, OBLIQUE, CROOKED, 'TRANSVERSE, *&c.* which have no immoral signification when applied to 'material shapes and figures, are nevertheless ODIOUS IN LAW, which 'is well observed by the great Sir Edward Coke.' "*Rectum*" (says he) "is a proper and significant word for "the RIGHT that any hath; and "WRONG, or INJURY, is in French "aptly called TORT, because INJURY "and WRONG is WRESTED or CROOK-"ED,

" ED, being contrary to that which is " *Right and Straight*," &c. (' See, in ' the margin below, the remainder of this ' Remark (18).

' But when great Nations become too ' subservient to *one*, or *a few individuals*, ' either by the corruption or total exclu- ' sion of *popular Representation*, in their re- ' spective Legislatures, they generally seem ' to lose all sense of *Right and Wrong*, all ' *common Honesty* in their political measures, ' as if they thought the command of an ' earthly superior would be a sufficient ' warrant for them to set aside THE ETER- ' NAL LAW, and so perpetrate the most ' abominable actions with impunity. How ' shall we account for such wretched

e ' *time-*

(18) —— " Now the LAW, that is" (says Sir Edward Coke) " LINEA RECTA *est Index sui et obliqui*. " And *Briton* saith that TORT A LA LEY EST CON- " TRARIE, and as aptly for the cause aforesaid is IN- " JURY, in English called WRONG. And INJU- " RIA is derived from *in* and *jus*, because it is con- " trary to RIGHT, so as *a faire tort* is *facere tortum*, " and *Fleta* saith, *est autem* JUS PUBLICUM *et* PRI- " VATUM *quod ex naturalibus præceptis aut Gentium*, " *aut civilibus, est collectum, et quod in jure scripto* JUS " *appellatur, id in lege* Angliæ RECTUM *esse dicitur*. " And in the *Mirror* and other places of the Law it " is called DROIT, as DROIT DEFEND, *the Law de-* " *fendeth*." 1 Inst. lib. 2. c. 12. p. 158. The last two words, however, ought rather to have been rendered *the Law forbiddeth*, than " *the Law defendeth*," because the English verb *defend* is very seldom used in the Sense which Sir Edward Coke meant to express.

'*time-serving*, in men who are endued 'with the *natural light* of *Reason* and '*Common Sense!* Perhaps it may be of- 'ten attributed to *the fear* of *temporal* '*Sufferings* and inconveniences which 'supercede that *Reason* and *Conscience* 'which should always controul the ac- 'tions of *Men*, and distinguish them from '*Brutes* (19). They forget that whilst 'they yield an implicit *active* obedience 'to the *unlawful* commands of any *tem-* '*poral Monarch* or *Legislature*, through 'the fear of present inconveniences or '*corporal Sufferings*, they rebel against 'the King eternal, who has power over 'their *souls* as well as their *bodies* (20).

'It was on this Principle alone; this 'sense of *superior Duty* arising from the 'fear of God, that I founded my Address 'to the *Gentlemen of the Army*, in my 'little

(19) For without these they deserve not the name of *men*, since a more evident "*mark of the Beast*" need not be sought for than the neglect of *reason* and *conscience*, or the baseness of yielding the same in an *active obedience* to the arbitrary *will* of any *man* or body of *men* whatsoever.

(20) "I say unto you," (said our Lord,) "my "friends, be not afraid of them that kill the body, "and, after that, have no more that they can do; but "I will forewarn you whom you shall fear: fear him, "which, after he hath killed, hath power to cast into "Hell; yea, I say unto you, fear him." Luke xii. 5. 6. See also Matthew x. 28.

' little Tract on " Crown Law, respect-
" ing the due distincton between *Murder*
" and *Manslaughter*;" but as my sentiments on that head have since been censured, I hope it will not be thought too foreign to my present topic, if I insist that no act of injustice can be more flagrant than that of denying to any particular order of Men (whether *Soldiers* or others) their *natural Right* of appealing to the *eternal Law*, and of acting agreeable to the dictates of their own *Reason* and *Conscience!*

In my former Tract I remarked, that " the Law will not excuse an *unlawful* " *Act committed by a* SOLDIER, even " though he commits it by *the express* " *Command* of the highest *military Autho-* " *rity* in the Kingdom," &c. and that " *Men of true Honour*," who have also " *a true Sense of Religion*, will not only " be mindful that they are *Soldiers* and " *Subjects* to an earthly KING, but that " they are also *Soldiers* and *Subjects* to the " KING of KINGS, whose Laws and " Precepts they will, on all occasions, " prefer to *every other command*," &c.

But this has been denied, it seems, by a Critic, in the Monthly Review for January, 1774, who calls it " *a strange Prin-* " *ciple!*" In an Age of infidelity, indeed, it may perhaps be allowed (in one Senſe) to be a *ſtrange Principle*; but then we have the greateſt Reaſon to lament the ignorance and depravity of thoſe Men who eſteem it ſo in any other ſenſe than that of being *too often* neglected and tranſgreſſed! for I truſt that no Man, who admits or believes the divine authority of the holy Scriptures, will doubt *the Truth of it.*

If this *ſtrange* PRINCIPLE had not been *equally true*, the Engliſh Nation (as I remarked in my former Tract) would long ago have been *enſlaved:* and I will now add, that even the very *ſtanding Army* itſelf would, by this time, have been reduced to that *abject State* of *political Slavery*, which at preſent diſgraces the *ſtanding Army* of *France* (21), and therefore

(21) I am a profeſſed enemy, indeed, to *ſtanding Armies*; but God forbid that I ſhould be ſo to the *individuals* incorporated therein, whoſe *true honour, natural dignity*, and *juſt privileges*, AS MEN, I ſhall ever be ready to aſſert and vindicate; and indeed I am bound to do ſo by that indiſpenſible duty which I owe to the great Author of *human Nature*, in oppoſition to the ſpiritual prince of this world, who is ever plotting to *corrupt, vilify*, and *enſlave*, that nobleſt work of God, *Mankind!* And as this ſame *Love* and *Regard*, which I here profeſs for the INDIVIDUALS *of the Army*, are certainly due alſo to the INDIVIDUALS *of every other Body of Men*, whoſe *general Principles* are cenſured in this Declaration, I muſt beg leave to aſſure my

fore those Writers, who attempt, by any fallacious sophistry, to withdraw our *British Soldiers* (22) from their obedience to the *eternal Law*, or from that allegiance which they indispensibly owe to the empire of *Reason* and *Conscience*, may justly be said to treat them more like *Brutes* than *Men!*

'But as all men of *Common Sense* are 'enabled, by that *hereditary Knowledge* 'beforementioned, (which has been *com-* '*mon* to all ranks of people ever since the 'fall of Man,) to distinguish *Good* '*from Evil* (23); so they are *equally* '*enabled* (and indeed *entitled*) thereby to '*judge* (24) concerning *the Legality of* '*all*

my Readers, that I do not mean to oppose the *Men*, but merely their *unreasonable Principles*, without any *personal* application whatsoever; for, otherwise, the severity of my expressions (especially against the *Church of Rome* and the *French Government*) would be entirely inconsistent with that "*Good-Will to Men*," which I am indispensibly obliged *, for my own eternal Happiness, to maintain!

(22) See Note in page x. of this *Preface*.

(23) This point is more particularly examined and proved in my Tract concerning, "*the Law of* "*Nature and Principles of Action in* MAN."

(24) "*Do ye not know that the Saints*" (which Term *is not confined to* Persons of any particular *Rank* or *Office*) "shall JUDGE THE WORLD? And, if "*the World shall be judged by you*, are ye *unworthy to* "*judge the smallest Matters?*—Know ye not that *we* "*shall* JUDGE *Angels?*—HOW MUCH MORE THINGS "THAT PERTAIN TO THIS LIFE." 1 Cor. vi. 2. 3.

* Upon this point I have wrote a distinct Tract, which is intended also for publication, and entitled "a Tract on the *Law of Liberty*."

'*all human Ordinances*, that is, to dif-
'cern and diftinguifh *Right* from *Wrong*,
'*Equity* from *Iniquity*, *Droit* from
'*Tort*, *Jus* from its oppofite *Injuria*,
'*&c.* This univerfal faculty of difcern-
'ment perhaps will be better known and
'more readily acknowledged under the
'title of *Confcience*; for by that natural
'inftinct of Confcience every individual
'*knows when he does amifs*, and is there-
'by rendered refponfible before God and
'Man for all his actions!

'And as all natural Faculties may be
'improved by the rudiments of Art and
'Science, fo even the NATURAL FEELINGS
'OF CONSCIENCE may be rendered more
'*fenfible*, *tender*, and *diftinguifhing*, by a
'proper Knowledge of *the Elements* or
'leading Precepts of the LAW ETERNAL.'

The remainder of the Tract confifts in a recital and application of fuch general *Maxims* as muft be allowed, by all perfons of *Common Senfe*, to be THE NECESSARY CONCLUSIONS OF REASON, and are therefore to be efteemed LAWS OF NATURE, fuch as *no Power on Earth can have any authority to counteract*; and the faid *general Maxims* or Rules of *Reafon* and *natural Law* are accordingly by our Law writers, with great propriety, efteemed the *firft Foundation of the Englifh Law.*

Law (25). It is on these incontrovertible and plain MAXIMS, these *necessary Conclusions* of REASON, that the following Declaration is founded; and therefore, as we are warned also by the revealed Laws of God "not to do *evil*, "that *good* may come (26)," every reasonable

(25) "Primum Fundamentum Legis Angliæ est LEX "RATIONIS, &c. Quæ *in hoc Regno*, sicut in omnibus aliis Regnis, ubique tenentur." Doct. et Stud. c. 5. p. 14. There is indeed an *inferior* order of *Maxims* (though yet of very great authority) which arise from general customs and the approved ancient determinations of the Courts of Law; and these form, what is called, THE FOURTH *foundation* of the *English Law*; though they may be ranked (as the Author of Doctor and Student informs us) with the *general ancient customs* on THE THIRD *foundation*. — "Si quis tamen pro "uno solo fundamento ea" (meaning *the general customs*, and the several *maxims* arising therefrom) "censeri "judicaverit, ad placitum suum, ea *pro uno tantum fundamento* compotare potest, et tunc secundum illum "*quinque fundamenta*" (for otherwise he reckons *six* in in all) "*Legis Angliæ tantum* assignari debent." Doct. et Stud. c. 8. p. 28. But as the true meaning of the said *inferior Maxims* is not *obvious* to people in general, like those belonging to the *first foundation*, it is happy for us that they are *not necessary* to be known by any persons who do not profess the Law; neither, indeed, can they be known without great study and labour, of which we are well apprised by the learned Author of Doctor and Student. "Hæc vero *maxima* solum in "Curiis Regiis, sive inter Legis Angliæ peritos nos-"cuntur, nec leviter absque *magno studio* in legibus "Angliæ habendo cognosci possunt. Ideo pro separabilibus fundamentis ponuntur. *Ibid.*

(26) The Apostle Paul has delivered a *most tremendous warning* to those wretched Politicians, who admit the baneful Doctrine — "*Let us do* EVIL *that* GOOD "*may*

ſonable Man muſt neceſſarily admit, that *Good* and *Evil*, *Right* and *Wrong*, *Juſtice* and *Iniquity*, can never change their real properties through the ſuppoſed NECESSITY of any political Meaſures whatſoever, and that nothing but *Juſtice* and *Righteouſneſs* can ever *eſtabliſh the Throne* (27) of our moſt gracious Sovereign, for whoſe Peace, and real Happineſs, both *temporal* and *eternal*, there is not a more ſincere wellwiſher amongſt all his Subjects, (notwithſtanding the freedom of the follow-Declaration,) than

GRANVILLE SHARP.

" *may come*;" for he immediately adds,—" WHOSE " DAMNATION" (ſays he) " IS JUST," Rom. iii. 8. If thoſe perſons, who contend for the ABSOLUTE NECESSITY *of Bribery*, *Penſions*, *and other* UNDUE *means of parliamentary Influence for the carrying on public Buſineſs*, would carefully conſider the ſaid *warning*, they would have juſt reaſon to be *alarmed* on account of their own *perſonal* danger, for having promoted ſuch a baneful and deſtructive principle!

(27) " Take away the Wicked from before the " King, and his *Throne* ſhall be *eſtabliſhed* in Righte- " ouſneſs." Prov. xxv. 5. It is only againſt ſome particular *Opinions* and *evil Council*, and not againſt the *Perſons* of thoſe who may have promoted the ſame, that I mean to apply this excellent proverb: The real intentions of ſuch Men, though *erroneous*, may have been *as ſincere* as my own; and I therefore proteſt, that my earneſt wiſh is to promote a *change* of *opinions* and *meaſures*, rather than of *perſons*, ſince thoſe, who are once convinced of their *former miſtakes*, may hereafter prove more uſeful Servants to the public than others perhaps, whoſe *abilities* and *conduct* are yet untried.

A DE-

A DECLARATION OF THE People's Natural Right to a Share in the Legislature, &c.

AN accurate and critical knowledge of Law (such as can only be acquired by much reading and long experience in the profession) is indeed a necessary qualification for those persons who undertake to deliver their opinions concerning the nicer and more difficult questions of jurisprudence; but, when the *Natural Rights* of any of our fellow-subjects are apparently at stake, every man has a right to judge for himself, and to declare his sentiments, as far as *plain conclusions of reason* and *common-sense* will fairly warrant; and ſuch only are referred to in the following Declaration of the *Natural Right* of popular Repreſentation in the legiſlature.*

" Amongſt all the rights and privileges " appertaining unto us," (ſaid that truly noble lawyer, Lord Sommers,) (1) " that " of having a Share in the Legiſlation, " and being to be governed by ſuch laws " as we ourſelves ſhall chuſe, is the moſt " fundamental and *eſſential*, as well as the moſt *advantageous* and beneficial, *&c.*"

And as all Britiſh ſubjects, whether in Great-Britain, Ireland, or the Colonies, are *equally free* by the law of *Nature*, they certainly are *equally* entitled to the ſame *Natural* Rights that are *eſſential* for their own preſervation; becauſe this privilege of " *having a ſhare in the legiſ-* " *lation*" is not merely a *Britiſh Right*, peculiar

(1) Judgement of whole Kingdoms, *&c.* p. 14.

culiar to *this island*, but it is alſo a *Natural Right*, which cannot, without the moſt flagrant and ſtimulating injuſtice, be withdrawn from any part of the Britiſh Empire *by any worldly authority whatſoever*; becauſe, "by the *natural Law*, "whereunto he [ALMIGHTY GOD] "hath made all ſubject," (ſays the learned Hooker,) (2) "the lawful power of "making laws, to command whole *politic ſocieties of men*, belongeth ſo properly *unto the ſame entire ſocieties*, that "for any Prince or Potentate, of *what kind ſoever* upon earth, to exerciſe the "ſame of himſelf," [or themſelves,] "and "not either by expreſs Commiſſion immediately and perſonally received from "God, or elſe by authority derived at the "firſt from *their conſent upon whoſe perſons they impoſe laws*, it is no better "than mere tyranny! Laws they are

 "not,

(2) Hooker's Eccleſiaſtical Polity, lib. 1, §. 10, p. 87.

" not, *therefore*, which public *Appro-* " *bation* hath not made ſo." Agreeable to the ſame juſt principles of *natural E-quity* is that maxim of the Engliſh Conſtitution, that " *Law, to bind all, muſt* " *be aſſented to by all*;" (Principia Leg. et Æquit. p.56.) and there can be no legal appearance of *Aſſent* without ſome degree of *Repreſentation*.

It muſt indeed be acknowledged, that the Repreſentation of the people of England is not ſo perfect as equity may ſeem to require, ſince very many individuals have no VOTE in Elections, and conſequently cannot be ſaid expreſſly to give *their Aſſent* to the laws by which they are governed: nevertheleſs, the whole country which they inhabit, and in which they earn their bread, and even the very houſes in which they live, (whether they are houſekeepers or lodgers,) are

are repreſented (3) by the votes of the reſpective proprietors; ſince *every Freeholder* has a *Right* to *vote*; ſo that, in this one reſpect, the Repreſentation is general; and, though *far from* EQUAL, would ſtill be a ſufficient check againſt arbitrary power, and afford ſufficient ſecurity for the lives and property of thoſe perſons who *have no Vote*, if the laws againſt parliamentary corruption (and eſpecially that Act of 7 and 8 Wil. III. c. 4.) were duly enforced; and alſo if all perſons, who are entruſted with the diſpoſal of public Money, were required to render a ſtrict account of it, and to be ſeverely puniſhed whenever convicted of exerting the influence of the *public treaſury* againſt *public liberty*; which is the moſt baneful treachery and diſhoneſty that men in office (who are the ſervants of

(3) I muſt beg leave to refer the reader alſo to ſome excellent obſervations on this head, in a Pamphlet publiſhed ſince the above was written, entitled, *An Argument in Defence of the Colonies*, p. 76, 77, and 78.

of *the Public*, as well as of *the King)* can poſſibly commit. But, notwithſtanding the *Inequality* of the Engliſh *Repreſentation*, and the various means practiſed to corrupt it, yet it has been the principal inſtrument of preſerving amongſt us thoſe remains of *natural Liberty* which we ſtill enjoy in a greater proportion than moſt other kingdoms, and has occaſioned more examples of juſt retribution on *Tyrants*, *Traitors*, and *Court-Favourites*, in the Engliſh annals, than the hiſtory of any other nation affords; ſo that M. Rapin is thereby led to conclude his account of K. Richard II. (that notorious corrupter of parliaments, and enemy to the privileges of London and other corporations) with the following reflection: " That, in a govern-" ment ſuch as that of England, all the " efforts that the Sovereign makes, to " uſurp an abſolute authority, are ſo " many ſteps which lead him towards " the

"the precipice." (4) It is manifeſt, therefore, that the conſtitutional government of England, even *with all its defects*, is infinitely better than any other form of government whereby *the people* are deprived of their juſt ſhare in the legiſlature; (5) ſo that the *Inequality* of *Repreſentation* in this iſland affords no juſt

(4) "C'eſt que dans un Gouvernement tel que "celui d'Angleterre, tous les efforts que le Souverain "fait pour uſurper un pouvoir abſolu ſont autant de "pas qui le conduiſent vers le précipice." Tome 3, Liv. x. p. 329.

(5) The celebrated Chancellor Forteſcue aſſerts, that a limited or politic Government (like that of England) is infinitely more eligible, for the intereſt and ſatiſfaction *even of the Prince himſelf*, than an abſolute regal power: —— "*Non jugum ſed libertas* eſt politicè "regere populum; *ſecuritas* quoque maxima nedum "plebi, ſed ET IPSI REGI; alleviatio etiam non mi-"nima ſolicitudinis ſuæ:" —— *Viz.* "That to rule "the people by Government politic is *no Yoke*, but "*Liberty*, and *great ſecurity*, not only to the ſubjects, "but *alſo to the King himſelf*; and further, no ſmall "lightening or eaſement to his charge." (De Laud. Leg. Angl. cap. 34, p. 78.) So that thoſe politicians, who plead the neceſſity of ſecuring, at any rate, a majority in parliament, to vote, implicitly for whatever the

juſt argument for ſetting aſide the *Repreſentation* of the people in other parts of the Britiſh Empire; becauſe experience teaches us, that even a *defective Repreſentation* is better than none at all; and therefore it is highly *unreaſonable*, and contrary to *natural Equity*, to pretend that our brethren and fellow-ſubjects in the more diſtant parts of the Britiſh Empire

pire

the Miniſter propoſes, do miſerably betray the true intereſt and peace of their Sovereign! for this fixes upon the King and his Miniſters (as in arbitrary governments) the blame and ignominy of every determination that happens to be wrong, which would otherwiſe either have been overruled by the free Council of the nation, or elſe muſt have been equally imputed to the People themſelves: and yet this wretched policy has alternately been adopted by all parties, notwithſtanding that it is founded (like many of Machiavel's doctrines) on that abominable antichriſtian principle of mere worldly-minded men, — "Let us do evil that good may come;" — "*whoſe damnation* (ſays the apoſtle to the Romans) *is juſt.*" Rom. iii. 8. The *evil* of an undue parliamentary influence they endeavour to excuſe by the plea of *Neceſſity* for the *Good* of the *State*, though it is certainly the moſt flagrant Violation of the fundamental principles of the *State*, and is abſolutely deſtructive of the true intereſt both of the *Prince* and *People!*

pire ought to be deprived *entirely* of their *natural Rights* and *Liberties*, merely because our own liberties *are not entirely perfect!* or becauſe our own Repreſentation in the Legiſlature appears, in ſome few reſpects, to be defective! and it would be quite as *unreaſonable* to alledge, that the principle or reaſon of the maxim before quoted (*viz.* that *Law, to bind all, muſt be aſſented to by all*) is unjuſt and inconcluſive, merely becauſe it would be very difficult to accompliſh it *literally* by the expreſs *aſſent* of every individual! But it is clearly ſufficient that the maxim be conſtrued to ſignify that *delegated aſſent* of the people by a majority of their *legal Repreſentatives*, which is *conſtitutionally* neceſſary to make *all laws binding*; (6) and ſuch a legal Repreſenta-

tion

(6) " Nedum principis voluntate, *ſed et totius regni* " *aſſenſu*, ipſa (*i. e.* Angliæ ſtatuta) conduntur, quo " populi læſuram illa efficere nequeunt, vel non eo-
" rum

tion of the people is therefore abſolutely neceſſary to conſtitute an *effectual Legiſlature* for any part of the *Britiſh Empire*; for no Tax can be levyed without manifeſt *Robbery and Injuſtice* where this *legal and conſtitutional Repreſentation* is wanting; becauſe the Engliſh Law abhors the idea of taking the leaſt property from *Freemen* without their *free conſent* — " It *is iniquitous*" (" *iniquum* " *eſt*," ſays the maxim) (7) " that *Free-* " *men*

" rum commodum procurare," &c. —— " Et ſi ſtatuta hæc, tanta ſolennitate et prudentia edita, efficaciæ tantæ, quantæ conditorum cupiebat intentio, non eſſe contingant, concito reformari ipſa poſſunt, et NON SINE COMMUNITATIS ET PROCERUM REGNI ILLIUS ASSENSU, quali ipſa primitus emanarunt," &c. Chancel. Forteſc. de Laud. Leg. Ang. c. 18, p. 40. b.

(7) " *Iniquum eſt* ingenuis hominibus non eſſe liberam rerum ſuarum alienationem." Co. Lit. 223. And again: " Quod noſtrum eſt, ſine facto ſive defectu noſtro, amitti ſeu in alium transferri non poteſt." 8 Co. 92. " Rerum ſuarum quilibet eſt moderator et arbiter." Co. Lit. 223. " Regulariter non valet pactum *de re mea* non alienanda." Co.

" *men* ſhould not have the *free* diſpoſal " of their *own effects*;" — and whatever is *iniquitous* can never be made *lawful* (8) by any authority on earth; not even by the united authority of King, Lords, and Commons; for that would be contrary to the *eternal* (9) *Laws of God*, which are ſupreme. (10)

In every point of view, the making laws for the ſubjects of any part of the Britiſh Empire, *without their participation and aſſent*, is INIQUITOUS, and therefore

Co. Lit. 223. And again: " Non poteſt rex ſubditum renitentem onerare impoſitionibus.' 2 Inſt. 61. from Forteſcue, c. 9. and 18.

(8) " Quicquid eſt contra normam recti eſt *injuria*." 3 Bulſ. 313. And " *Lex* nemini operatur " *iniquum* — nemini facit *injuriam*." Jenk. Cent. 22. And therefore " Quod *contra legem fit* PRO INFECTO " *habetur*." 4 Co. 31.

(9) " *Lex eſt ab æterno*." Jenk. Cent. 34.

(10) — " Etiam ſi aliquod ſtatutum eſſet editum " contra eas," (leges divinas,) " *nullius vigoris* in legibus Angliæ *cenſeri debet*," *&c*. Doct. et Stud. c. 6, p. 18.

fore *unlawful :* for though the purport of any law, ſo made, be in itſelf perfectly *juſt* and *equitable*, yet it becomes otherwiſe (11) (that is, *unjuſt* and *iniquitous*, and therefore *unlawful)* by the want of theſe neceſſary *legal Formalities* (12) of *Repreſentation* and *Aſſent :* for if the inhabitants of *one part* of the empire might determine a queſtion, or enact a law, for the peculiar advantage only of that *one part*, though to the manifeſt detriment and injury of *another part*, without the *Repreſentation* of the latter, the former part would be made *judges in their own cauſe* ; a circumſtance that would be literally *partial !* the very reverſe of juſtice and *natural equity*, and which muſt, therefore, be eſteemed *Iniquity*,

(11) " Qui aliquid ſtatuerit *parte inaudita altera*, æ-" quum licet dixerit, *haud æquum fecerit*." Princip. Leg. et Æquit. p. 90. or — " *haud æquus fuerit*." 6 Co. 52.

(12) " *Forma legalis* forma *eſſentialis*." 10. Co. — 100. And " *Forma* non obſervata *infertur adnullatio* " *actus*." 12 Co. 7.

iquity, even to a fundamental maxim, (13) *viz.* "It is INIQUITOUS for any one to "*be a Judge in his own cause.*" *Partiality* is, therefore, ſuch an abomination in the eye of the law, that no Power on earth can make it LAWFUL: for "even "*an Act of Parliament*" (ſays the learned Judge Hobart, Rep. 87.) "made a-"gainſt NATURAL EQUITY, as to *make* "*a man judge in his own caſe,*" (the example, obſerve, is the very point in queſtion) "*is* VOID *in itſelf*;" for "jura na-"turæ ſunt immutabilia," and they are "leges legum."

Every King of England (apparently for the *ſame reaſon)* is reſtrained by the Law from changing or *making new Laws* "without the aſſent or conſent of his "WHOLE KINGDOM in *Parliament ex-* "*preſſed.*

(13) "Iniquum eſt aliquem rei ſui eſſe judi-"cem." — "In propria cauſa nemo judex." Principia Legis et Æquitatis, p. 41.

" *preſſed*. (14) And the *whole Kingdom*, even of *Great-Britain* itſelf, is only *a part* of the *Britiſh Empire*; and therefore, by a parity of reaſoning, cannot *juſtly* or *equitably* be permitted to make laws for *the whole*; becauſe " where " the ſame *reaſon is*, the ſame law (or " right) muſt prevail:" (15) for " turpis eſt " *pars* quæ non convenit cum ſuo *toto*;" (Plowden, 161.) and " nihil in lege *in-* " *tolerabilius* eſt, eandem rem *diverſo* " *jure* cenſeri." 4 Co. 83. The free Repreſentation of the *people in the legiſlature* is, therefore, to be eſteemed, of all our Rights, the *moſt eſſential*, (as Lord Sommers has declared,) to maintain that excellent Equilibrium of power, or mixt government, *limited by law*, which our anceſtors

(14) " Neque Rex ibidem, per ſe, aut miniſtros " ſuos, tallagia, ſubſidia, aut quævis onera alia, im- " ponit legiis ſuis, aut *leges eorum mutat*, *vel novas con-* " *dit*, *ſine conceſſione* vel *aſſenſu totius regni ſui in parlia-* " *mento ſuo expreſſo*," *&c.* Chancell. Forteſcue de Laudibus Legum Angliæ, c. 36, p. 84. b.

(15) " Ubi eadem ratio, ibi idem lex," *or* " jus." Principia Leg. et Æquit. p. 116.

anceſtors have always moſt zealouſly aſſerted, and tranſmitted to us, as our beſt *Birthright* and *Inheritance*; (16) ſo that every attempt *to ſet the ſame aſide* in any degree, or in any *part of the empire*, or to *corrupt it* by undue influence of places and penſions, or bribes with public money, is *Treaſon againſt the Conſtitution*; the higheſt of Treaſon: (17) and therefore

(16) "Major hæreditas venit unicuique noſtrum a "jure et legibus quam a parentibus." 2 Inſt. 56.

(17) "The *firſt and higheſt Treaſon* is that which is "committed *againſt the Conſtitution*." Lord Sommers's Judgement of whole Kingdoms, p. 8. — "Eſt autem "*injuria* omne quod non *jure* fit." Fleta, l. 2, c. 1. And, on the other hand, "they neither are, nor can "be Traitors, who endeavour to preſerve and maintain the Conſtitution; but they are the Traitors, "who deſign and purſue the ſubverſion of it; they "are the Rebels, that go about to overthrow the Government of their Country; whereas ſuch as ſeek "to ſupport and defend it are the *truly loyal perſons*, "and do act conformable to the ties and obligations of "fealty." Lord Sommers, p. 9. — Agreeable to this doctrine was the anſwer of Dr. Sharp, archbiſhop of York, when the queſtion was put to him, "How a perſon, who had ſworn Allegiance to King James, "could,

fore whatſoever is ordained, that can clearly be proved to be *contrary to the conſtitution*, muſt be allowed to be *fundamentally wrong*, and therefore *null* and *void* of itſelf; for, " ſublato fundamento, " cadit opus." (Jenk. Cent. 106.) But more particularly the Parliament has no power

" could, with a good conſcience, take the ſame oath " to King William ?" To which he replied, " That " the Laws of the land are the only rule of our con-" ſcience in this matter, and we are no further bound " to pay obedience to governors, nor to any other go-" vernors, than the Laws enjoin. If, therefore, King " William, in the eye of the Law, be our King, we muſt " in conſcience pay obedience to him as ſuch. I take " this" (ſays he) " for a certain truth, that, *as the* " *Law makes the King*, ſo the ſame *Law* extends, or " limits, or *transfers*, our obedience and allegiance; " and all Oaths impoſed by the Law oblige the con-" ſcience no further than the Law meant they ſhould " oblige. Only this is always to be remembered, " that whatever Obedience the Laws of the land re-" quire of us, it is to be underſtood with this proviſo, " that it be not contradictory to the Laws of God. " But in that caſe we muſt obey paſſively, though we " cannot obey actively: and with this tacit condition " I do ſuppoſe all oaths of fidelity in the world are " given and taken." Life of Abp. Sharp, part 3d, pag. 24, 25, and 26. MS. wrote by his Son, for the uſe of his Grandchildren.

power to give up the ancient and established Right of the *people* to be *represented* in the *legislature* ; because an Act for so base a purpose would entirely subvert the principles and constitution on which the very Existence of the legislature itself, which ordained it, is formed! so that such an *unnatural Act* of the state would be parallel to the crime of *felo de se* in a private person ; and, being thus contrary to " *the nature* of things, " can never be *rendered valid* by any " Authority whatsoever." (18) And indeed it is laid down as a maxim, by the great Lord Sommers, that " no man or " society of men have *power to deliver* " *up their preservation*, or the means of " it, to the *absolute Will* of any man" (or men) ; " and they will have always " a right to preserve what they have not

D " power

(18) " Quæ rerum naturâ prohibentur NULLA " LEGE confirmata sunt." (Finch, 74.) And " Nihil " quod est *contra rationem* est licitum." Co. Lit. 97.

"power to part with." P. 26. And if a politic ſociety has no juſt power to deliver up even *its own* preſervation, it certainly has *much leſs right* to deliver up the neceſſary preſervation of other ſocieties of their brethren and friends (not repreſented among them) *without their Conſent:* and all ſuch attempts muſt neceſſarily be deemed *void* and ineffectual, becauſe "there is no neceſſity to obey, where "there is *no authority* to ordain." (19) For as it ſo clearly appears, from what has been ſaid, that *Natural Equity* does not permit even *the inferior Property* of lands, *goods*, chattels, or money, to be alienated without the *conſent* or *fault* of the proprietors, much leſs can it permit the alienation, annulling, or changing, of our *moſt valuable inheritance, the Law*, without the *due aſſent and conſent* of *the heritors*

(19) "Ubi non eſt condendi authoritas, ibi non eſt "parendi neceſſitas." Dav. 69. And "Judicium a "non ſuo judice datum nullius eſt momenti." 10 Co. 76.

heritors themselves, the People at large, or their lawful Representatives in their respective assemblies or parliaments! (20) This is a necessary conclusion of *reason and common-sense*, drawn from the effect and force of *Natural Equity*, even in cases of much less consequence (*viz.* respecting goods and common pecuniary property); so that the distinction, which some great and able politicians have lately made, between *Taxation* and *Legislation*, (in the late disputes about taxing the Colonies,) was certainly *erroneous*, though well intended; since it plainly appears, that the right of *Legislation* is not less

(20) " Nam non potest rex Angliæ, ad *libitum suum*, " *leges mutare regni* sui. Principatu namque nedum " *regali*, sed et *politico*, ipse suo populo dominatur." And again: " Quia nec leges, ipse" [rex] " sine " *subditorum assensu mutare poterit*, nec *subjectum populum renitentem onerare impositionibus peregrinis*; quare " populus ejus *libere fruetur bonis suis*, LEGIBUS, *quas* " *cupit*, *regulatus*, nec per regem suum, *aut quemvis* " *alium depilatur*," &c. Chancel. Fortescue de Laud. Leg. Ang. c. 9, p. 26.

inseparable, by *Natural Equity*, from the people of every part of the British Empire, than the right of *granting or with-holding Taxes*; for, otherwise, the free subjects of *one part* of the empire would be liable to be most materially injured in their *greatest* and most valuable inheritance, *the Law*, by the hasty decisions of men on the *other side of* the empire, with whom probably they would be totally unacquainted, and whose interest might perhaps be as widely *different* from theirs (for any thing they could know to the contrary) as their *situation* upon the face of the globe *is distant*; that is, as widely *different as the East is from the West!* Would this be equitable? could such notorious *Injustice* (21) be

(21) "Si a *jure* discedas, vagus eris, et erunt omnia omnibus incerta." Co. Lit. 227. And, "Rerum ordo confunditur si *unicuique jurisdictio non servetur*." (4 Inst. proem.) For, if the fundamental Rule of the Constitution be set aside even in *one instance*,

be ever made lawful? The true constitutional mode of *connecting* British Dominions, that are otherwise separated by *Nature*, is demonstrated by the established example of the Union of Great-Britain and Ireland, which by long experience has proved to be sufficiently effectual. It must be acknowledged, indeed, that an Act of Parliament was made in the 6th of K. George I. chap. 5. wherein it is laid down, that "the King "and Parliament of Great-Britain *may* "*make Laws to bind Ireland*." (22) But, as

instance, the baneful influence of such an evil precedent will soon prepare the way for the *Destruction of the whole Law*; because "*uno absurdo dato, infinita* "*sequuntur*." 1 Coke, 102.

(22) If the preceding arguments are not sufficient to prove in what light the said Act is to be considered, yet the present *distinct and separate Jurisdiction* of *the Irish Parliament*, the Continuation of their *ancient* and *constitutional Privileges*, notwithstanding the doctrine asserted in the said Act, and their annual Transactions, both in *Taxation* and *Legislation*, are *Facts*, which prove (*better than Arguments*) that the people of Ireland

as it does not appear that the Parliament of Ireland ever acknowledged or gave any

land have an inherent Right to enact Laws independent of the British Parliament; otherwise the King's *Assent* would not be sufficient to render the said laws *valid and binding* without the especial approbation and consent also of the British Parliament, which indeed is *never required*; *so far is it from being necessary!* And, farther, the inhabitants of Great-Britain would think it extremely unreasonable and unjust, if the Parliament of Ireland should claim a Right of making Laws, with the King's assent, to *bind any part of this Island!* The argument is reciprocal: so that, if we should really detest such a measure against ourselves, *the Law of Laws* forbids us to claim the like power over any of our fellow-subjects, without their free consent. "*Non facias alteri quod tibi non vis fieri.*" This is laid down as one of the most common precepts of the *Law of Reason* (Doct. and Stud. c. 2, p. 7.); and such is the immutability of the *Law of Reason*, that against it there can be no *prescription*, *statute*, or *custom*; and if any are made contrary thereto, they are not to be esteemed *statutes* or *customs*, but *corruptelæ*, *i. e.* Corruptions or Depravities — "Non sunt statuta sive consuetudines, sed *corruptelæ*." Doct. and Stud. c. 2, p. 5. To the same effect is that Command of Christ himself, (recorded in Matt. vii. 12.) which our Lord declared to be "*the Law and the Prophets*;" viz. "*Whatsoever ye would that men should do to you, do ye even so to them: for this is* THE LAW AND THE PROPHETS": so that it may justly be intitled, the *Law of Laws*; and a statute, therefore, which is contrary thereto, is *doubly unlawful*.

The

any *formal Assent* to the said Act, the same must necessarily be considered as a *mere*

The separate interests of the two Kingdoms are sufficiently restrained, with respect to each other, by our excellent Constitution of State, which requires *the Assent of the People*, (that is of those which are concerned respectively,) to render any *Law valid* and *binding* upon either nation; which the foregoing arguments demonstrate: and I hope the ingenious and sensible author of the argument in defence of the Colonies (lately published) will acknowledge, that he has allowed too much, when he admits, in page 114, that "*the whole kingdom of Ireland is bound by the Acts of the* "*supreme Legislature*, &c." which doctrine leads him afterwards to make a distinction between Taxation and Legislation.

And again, the two kingdoms are so firmly united, by the *bands of Allegiance*, to *one Head* (or Monarchy) of *limited power*, that their interests in all material *external* exigences are thereby *rendered mutual*, as well as their *internal* interest, in the maintenance of *natural* and *constitutional Liberty*, in each kingdom respectively; because one of them cannot be deprived of this, (as they are governed by *the same Head*,) without hastening the destruction of the other. And this intimate connexion of *mutual interest* in the constitution of state, and in the reciprocal enjoyment of the *same reasonable common Law*, (whereby each kingdom enjoys an Equality of privilege, and natural freedom,) renders the Union of the two kingdoms *more just and equitable*, and, consequently, *more safe and durable*, than *mere aſſertion* on *one part*, at the making of which, the perſons moſt materially concerned on *the other part* were neither HEARD, *nor repreſented!* a defect (23) the moſt notorious that can poſſibly be attributed to any proceeding, either in the *enacting* or *execution of Laws!* and therefore it is to very little purpoſe to cite the ſaid Act as a Precedent for taxing the American Subjects *without their Conſent*; for

than it could poſſibly have been made by any other means: and the inhabitants of both iſlands (though ſprung from a variety of jarring, jealous, and fierce nations) have, by theſe means acquired a certain *mutual conſideration* for each other, as *fellow-ſubjects*, which could never have been produced by mere alliances, guarantees, or defenſive leagues, nor, perhaps, by any other mode of government whatever, than that by which divine Providence has effected it; *viz.* the Engliſh Conſtitution: this has firmly united the *Strength* of the two Iſlands; whereby reciprocal ſuccour, in time of need, is inſured to both.

(23) "Qui aliquid ſtatuerit, parte *inaudita altera*, "licet æquum dixerit, *haud æquum* fecerit:" ſo that, if any act is ever ſo juſt in itſelf, yet it becomes *otherwiſe* (that is, *unjuſt and iniquitous*, as is before remarked) by the want of theſe legal formalities.

for the privileges which the Parliament of Ireland has maintained and enjoyed, both before and ſince that time, (clearly diſtinct and ſeparate from the Britiſh Parliament,) afford a better and more authentic precedent on the *other ſide of the queſtion, (viz.* in behalf of the people's *natural Rights,)* than the Act itſelf does againſt them: for, as the King and the People (including the Lords and Commons) of Great-Britain conſtitute the *ſovereign Power* (under God) or Legiſlature of Great-Britain, ſo the King and the People of Ireland are the natural and conſtitutional Legiſlature or State of that kingdom, and actually exerciſe (both in *Legiſlation and Taxation)* their diſtinct juriſdiction, to this day; which is the beſt proof of their Right: and, in like manner, according to this ancient and eſtabliſhed legal precedent, the King, together with the People of every diſtinct province, ſubject to the imperial

Crown of Great-Britain, and detached (as Ireland is) from this iſland, ought to be and have been eſteemed, from the firſt eſtabliſhment of our colonies, the only proper and conſtitutional Legiſlature for *each province reſpectively*; (24) becauſe the *Repreſentation of the People*, in every part of the Britiſh Empire, is abſolutely neceſſary to conſtitute an *effectual Legiſlature*, according to the fundamental principles of the Engliſh Conſtitution; for none of them, *ſeparately*, can

(24) Every eſtabliſhment in the American Colonies has been ſettled by our anceſtors as nearly as poſſible to the conſtitutional form of government in the Mother-Country; and, as the advantages of this mode have been proved by the experience of more than a century; (ſee an argument, juſt publiſhed, in defence of the excluſive Right, claimed by the Colonies, to tax themſelves, p. 36, 39, 44.) it is very dangerous (now that the colonies begin to be filled with people) to vary the ancient and approved Form of the Conſtitution. "*Periculoſum eſt res novas et inuſitatas inducere.*" Co. Lit. 379. And, "Clauſulæ inconſuetæ "ſemper inducunt ſuſpicionem." 3 Co. 81. And again, "Quæ præter conſuetudinem et morem majorum "fiunt neque placent, neque recta videntur." 4 Co. 78. And laſtly, "Whatſoever is againſt the Rule of "Law is inconvenient." Co. Lit. p. 379.

can be eſteemed a *competent Legiſlature* to judge of the other's *Rights*, without the higheſt injuſtice and *iniquity*; which is before demonſtrated by ſome of the firſt maxims or principles of *Reaſon*. And yet, howſoever diſtinct theſe ſeveral parts or provinces may ſeem, in point of ſituation, as well as in the exerciſe of a ſeparate legiſlative power for each, (which conſtitutional Right they have enjoyed beyond the memory of man,) they are nevertheleſs firmly united by the circle of the Britiſh Diadem, ſo as to form *one vaſt Empire*, which will never be divided, if the ſafe and honeſt policy be adopted, of maintaining the *Britiſh Conſtitution* inviolate, in all parts of the Empire: for it is a ſyſtem ſo *natural*, ſo *beneficial*, and ſo *engaging*, to the generality of mankind, that by the ſame means we might hold *the Empire of the World*, were the laws of natural Equity, Juſtice, and Liberty, to be ſtrictly obſerved, and the *abomination* of *domeſtic* (25) as well as political Slavery aboliſhed!

On the other hand, it is not only *Treaſon againſt the Conſtitution* to attempt to deprive any free Britiſh Subjects of their *natural Right* to a Share in the *Legiſlature*, (26) but it is equally derogatory and injurious to the Authority of the Crown; (27) becauſe a King of England

(25) The toleration of domeſtic Slavery in the Colonies greatly weakens the claim or *natural Right* of our American Brethren to Liberty. Let them put away *the accurſed thing* (that horrid *Oppreſſion*) from among them, before they preſume to implore the interpoſition of *divine Juſtice*; for, whilſt they retain their *brethren of the world* in the moſt ſhameful involuntary ſervitude, it is profane in them to look up to the *merciful* Lord of all, and call him *Father*!

(26) " To extend the Governor's Right to com- " mand, and Subject's Duty to obey, beyond the " Laws of one's country," (ſaid that learned lawyer, Lord Sommers,) " is TREASON againſt the Conſtitu- " tion, and Treachery to the ſociety whereof we are " members." Judgement of whole Kingdoms, *&c.* p. 6.

(27) " Nor is it merely the firſt and higheſt *Treaſon* " in *itſelf*, that a member of a political ſociety is ca- " pable

land has no *legal Authority* to govern by any other mode than that *limited* government called the *English Constitution*, which he is ſworn to maintain; for ſuch is the frailty of human nature, that no man or body of men whatever is to be entruſted with the adminiſtration of government, unleſs they are *thus limited by Law*, and by a due Repreſentation of the people at large, ſubject to a frequent appeal, *by Election*, to the whole body of conſtituents: for it is a maxim, "that "he who is allowed *more Power, by* "*Law*, than is fit, (or equitable,) the "ſame will ſtill deſire more Power than

"is

"pable of committing, *to go about to ſubvert the Con-* "*ſtitution*; but it is alſo the *greateſt Treaſon* he can "perpetrate againſt the *Perſon, Crown, and Dignity* "*of the King*; for ſuch an endeavour both annuls "and vacates all his title to ſuperiority over thoſe "above whom he was exalted from the common le- "vel by *virtue of the Conſtitution*, and deprives him "of all rightful and legal claim of rectoral au- "thority over the ſociety, by deſtroying the alone "foundation upon which it was erected, and by "which he became veſted with it," *&c.* Ibid. p. 9 & 10.

" is already *lawful* :" (28) so that no Power on earth is tolerable without a *just limitation*; and Law, which ought to be supreme, (29) cannot subsist where *Will* and *Pleasure* are absolute, whether it be the *Will* of *one*, of a *few*, or of *many*. (30)

A King, therefore, who presumes to act without the constitutional *limitation*, destroys the foundation of his *own authority*; for the most respectable and most ancient writer on the English Constitution assures us, that " *there is no* " *King* where *Will rules*," (or is *absolute*,)

(28) " Cui plus licet quam *par* est, *plus vult* quam " licet." 2 Inst. 465.

(29) " Firmior et potentior est *operatio legis* quam " dispositio hominis." Co. Lit. 102.

(30) " Whosoever" (says Aristotle) " is governed " by a man *without Law*, is governed by a *man and* " *by a beast*." Lord Sommers, N. 11.

" Ipse autem rex, non debet esse sub homine, sed *sub* " *Deo*, *et sub lege*; *quia lex facit regem*. Attribuat " igitur rex *legi* quod *lex* attribuit ei, videlicet *domi-* " *nationem*

lute,) " and not *Law.*" (31) The ſame doctrine is expreſſed ſtill more clearly in the old Year Books, (32) that, " if " there was *no Law*, there would be " *no King*, and no inheritance."

For theſe plain reaſons, whenever the Engliſh Government ceaſes *to be limited*, in any part of the Britiſh Dominions, it ceaſes to be *lawful!*

And therefore the fatal conſequences of proceeding to enforce the execution of any Acts, or Reſolutions, for the eſ-tabliſhing

" *nationem et poteſtatem : non eſt enim rex ubi dominatur* " *voluntas, et non lex.*" Bracton, lib. 1, c. 8. —— " Rex autem habet ſuperiorem, Deum. S. —— *Item* " *legem, per quam factus eſt rex.* — Item curiam ſuam, " &c. —— Et ideo ſi rex fuerit *ſine fræno*, i. e. *ſine* " *lege*, debent ei frænum ponere," *&c.* Bract. lib. 2, c. 21, p. 34

(31) — " *Non eſt enim rex* ubi *dominatur voluntas*, et " *non lex.*" Bract. lib. 1, c. 8, p. 5, b.

(32) " — La *ley* eſt le plus haute inhéritance que " le roy ad : car par la *ley* il même et touts ſes ſu-" jets ſont rulés, et *ſi le ley ne fuit*, NUL ROI, *et nul* " *inhéritance, ſera.*" 19 Hen. VI. 63.

tablishing such *unlimited and unlawful* (33) Government, is more easily conceived than expressed; because " the " condition of all subjects would be a- " like, whether under *absolute* or *limited* " Government, if it were not *lawful* (34) " to maintain and preserve those limita- " tions, since *Will* and *Pleasure*, and not " Law, would be, alike in both, the *mea-* " *sure of obedience*; for, to have liberties " and privileges, unless they may be de- " fended, and to have *none at all*, is the " same thing as to be governed by *mere* " *Will and Pleasure*" (Lord Sommers, p. 24.); and " misera est *servitus* ubi jus " est vagum aut incertum."

(33) " Ubi non est *condendi authoritas*, ibi non est " parendi necessitas." Dav. 69. Prin. Leg. et Æquit. p. 117.

(34) " Insuper lex rationis permittit plurima fieri, " ut scilicet quod *licitum* est *vim vi* repellere, et quod " fas unicuique se tueri et *rem suam defendere contra* " *vim injustam*." Doct. et Stud. c. 2, p. 8. — See also Bracton, lib. 4, c. 4, p. 162. b.

Old-Jewry, London, June 25, 1774. GRANVILLE SHARP.

(C O P Y.)

EXTRACT of a LETTER on the foregoing Subject, to a Friend in AMERICA, dated February 21, 1774.

* * * * * * * * *

* * * * * * * * *

* * * * * * * * *

I have alſo ſent you a book lately publiſhed by Dr. ——, reſpecting the government of the Britiſh Colonies.

The reaſon of my ſending the latter is not becauſe I approve of it, or have the leaſt connexion with the author; but, on the contrary, that you and your friends in America may be aware of the unconſtitutional doctrines which are thereby propagated amongſt us. I have not, indeed, had opportunity to peruſe it regularly; neither do I now think it neceſſary to do ſo; for I was lucky enough, when I firſt took it up, to turn over a few pages in the fourth part, containing five propoſitions upon the point in queſtion, whereby the author's ſentiments and intentions may be ſufficiently known without deſcending to his arguments upon them; for *not one* of them (not even the 5th and laſt, which he himſelf prefers) can poſſibly be reconciled either to *Law*, *Equity*, or *ſound Politicks*; ſo that if the doctor, with the *ſame neglect of Law and conſtitutional Principles*, had multiplied his propoſitions to the number of *an hundred times five*, he would not have been able to lay down a plan or mode

mode of government tolerably ſuitable to the caſe before him; becauſe, in this, as in many other things, there is but *one right*, though very many *wrong* methods of proceeding; and the doctor has unfortunately forgot to ſtate the *only right propoſition* upon the ſubject in queſtion, that can be admitted conſiſtently with the neceſſary principles abovementioned of *Law*, *Equity*, *and ſound Politicks*; viz. to *do juſtice* to our brethren of America; that is, to govern them according to the eſtabliſhed Principles of the Engliſh Conſtitution, and known Laws of the Land, and candidly to acknowledge their *unalienable* right to the ſame happy privileges by which the liberties of the mother-country have hitherto been maintained; the moſt eſſential of which is the privilege of paying no other taxes than what are voluntarily granted by *the people* or their *legal repreſentatives* in general councils or parliaments.

Dr. —— is inexcusable for having omitted this *sixth Proposition!* for he cannot be ignorant of the legal and *established mode of extending the English Constitution to countries detached from this island*, because we have a standing precedent and example (which has long subsisted, and has been universally allowed) in the present government of *Ireland*; for that island, though unjustly *conquered* by our ancestors, enjoys (or, at least, is allowed to be entitled to) the same constitutional privileges as the seat of empire, England itself. The respective Parliaments of the two islands are *entirely independent of each other*; they *separately* grant, from time to time, the necessary supplies to the state; and no man may presume to deny their right of enquiring respectively into the application of them. But, notwithstanding this distinct œconomy, and the entire independency of the natives or subjects,

ſubjects, with reſpect to each other, yet they are firmly united, by the *bands of allegiance*, to *one* Head (or Monarchy) of *limited power*, whereby they enjoy the privileges of the *ſame reaſonable common Law*, and the *ſame excellent Conſtitution* of ſtate: ſo that the equality of *privilege* and *condition* renders the *Union* more juſt and equitable, and conſequently more ſafe and durable, than it could poſſibly have been made by any other means.

And the inhabitants of both iſlands (though ſprung from a variety of jarring, jealous, and fierce nations) have, by this means, acquired a certain *mutual conſideration* for each other, as *fellow-ſubjects*, which could never have been produced by mere alliances, guarantees, or defenſive leagues, nor perhaps by any other mode of government whatever, than that by which Divine Providence has effected it; *viz.* the Engliſh Conſtitution.

This

This has firmly united the *ſtrength* of the two iſlands; whereby reciprocal ſuccour in time of need is inſured to both. This *eſtabliſhed example* of the true conſtitutional mode of connecting Britiſh Dominions, that are otherwiſe ſeparated by Nature, will enable us, by compariſon, to diſcern the illegality and injuſtice of Dr. ——'s five Propoſitions. The ſtately vine of Britiſh Dominion (if I may uſe that ſcriptural type) has providentially extended its luxuriant branches to the moſt diſtant parts of the earth! and will continue to ſpread and increaſe as long as *Juſtice* and *the Laws of Liberty* are duly maintained by thoſe who are entruſted with the adminiſtration of government (unleſs the wickedneſs of *individuals*, manifeſted by the exerciſe of *domeſtic Slavery* and *Oppreſſion* in the Colonies, and of *political Corruption and Venality* at home, with the *growing vices* attending

attending *both* reſpectively, ſhould unhappily draw down God's vengeance upon us! and perhaps our mutual puniſhment is at this time impending in the preſent differences and ignorance of the Engliſh Conſtitution): But how will the trunk or ſtock of the Britiſh Vine appear, if we ſhould entirely ſeparate or lop off the branches? — The American Branches are already *detached*, indeed, (in point of diſtance,) and widely ſeparated from the Trunk, by a vaſt Ocean; but the imperial Crown of Great-Britain is, nevertheleſs, a ſufficient band of union or connexion between them, it being the legal enſign of authority for the maintenance and execution of the ſame juſt laws, the influence of which may, by a due conſtitutional exertion of the regal Power, be circulated, like wholeſome ſap, from the root to the moſt diſtant branches.

But

But if (according to Dr. ——'s 5th propofition) the flourifhing branches of North-America were to be *entirely feparated* from the trunk, and excluded from the *circle* of the royal *diadem*, the effect would be *reciprocally humiliating*; for the act of feparation would, at the fame time, unavoidably *contract* the *imperial Authority of the Britifh Empire* to the narrow limits of Britifh and Irifh ground, except a few fmall Sugar-Iflands, peopled chiefly by the moft miferable of flaves: fo that both *Great-Britain* and her *Colonies* would reciprocally lofe *importance*, *ftrength*, and *fecurity*, by the difunion. A Guarantee of independence againft all foreign invaders, as propofed by Dr. ——, would fall far fhort of the effect which we enjoy by the prefent conftitution, becaufe it would not, like the latter, produce that *mutual confideration and protection* which are due from

fellow-

fellow-subjects. Our connexion, according to the doctor's measure, would be upon no better footing than Alliances of the same kind with detached foreign Powers, which (as experience teaches us) subsist no longer than the *private interest* or *separate* views of the contracting parties.

If all these points are duly considered, the very proposing so pernicious a measure must appear highly criminal, if not treasonable! especially as the author has been pleased to insinuate, that there is no alternative! — "If we neither can "govern the Americans," (says he,) "nor be governed by them; if we can "neither unite with them, nor ought "to subdue them; what remains" (says he) "but to part with them on as friendly "terms as we can?" But is it not Treason against the Crown to insinuate that the Americans cannot be *governed*, as well as Treaſon againſt the People at large, to ſay that we cannot *unite* with our American Brethren, when there is a conſtitutional mode both of *Government* and *Union*, eſtabliſhed by law, and an unqueſtionable precedent, the obſervance of which would undoubtedly ſatisfy every honeſt American Subject ?

The advocates for the juriſdiction of the Britiſh *Parliament in America*, like all promoters of bad meaſures, will not fail to repreſent thoſe, that oppoſe them, as licentious and diſaffected perſons ; and therefore, as it is highly neceſſary for the general *welfare* and ſubſiſtence of the Britiſh Empire, both in Europe, Aſia, and America, (upon the principles already explained,) that we ſhould ſtrictly maintain our *Loyalty to the Crown*, at the ſame time that we ſteadily aſſert our legal and conſtitutional Rights,— I think we ought to loſe no proper opportunity of of expreſſing our *perſonal attachment* to the *King and the royal Family*, who, in themſelves, indeed are truly amiable, and worthy of eſteem; but it is very difficult, in this world, to guard againſt miſrepreſentation and bad advice; however, I truſt that a ſteady perſeverance in *Love and Duty* will be the true means of your prevailing in the end, as it will prove that your oppoſition is not occaſioned either by diſaffection or diſloyalty, but is *truly legal* and *conſtitutional*.

* * * * * *

* * * * * *

I am, with great eſteem,

Dear Sir,

Your obliged humble Servant,

GRANVILLE SHARP.

P.S. I am entirely unacquainted, I profefs, with the nature of the Crown Charters or Grants to the feveral American Proprietors; and therefore (left thefe fhould contain any condition or acknowledgement, on the part of the landholders, which may feem to militate againft the foregoing obfervations) I muft beg leave to add, that the legiflature hath agreed and laid down, as a rule, that all the ancient arbitrary and military Tenures of land, and even "Socage *in capite* of the "King, and the *confequents upon the* "*fame*, have been much more burthen-"fome, *grievous, and prejudicial, to the* "*Kingdom, than they have been beneficial* "*to the King*" (fee preamble to the Act of 12th of Charles II. chap. 24, for taking away *the Court of Wards and Liveries and Tenures in capite, and by Knights Service and Purveyance*, &c.); and for this juft reafon, founded on "*former*

"*expe-*

" *experience,** the Crown hath ever ſince been reſtrained by the Law from *granting* " *any Manors*, Lands, *&c.*" upon ſuch, or indeed *any other conditions whatſoever*, than " *free and common Socage only.*"†

I have heard, indeed, that a certain iſland in the northern part of America was granted to a noble lord, with a particular juriſdiction upon the ancient feudal plan, whereby he is ſaid to have been eſtabliſhed as *Lord Paramount*, with a peculiar unconſtitutional authority: but this, I am willing to preſume, is merely report; and, even if it were true, the Grant would be innocent enough in its effects,

* Whereas it hath been found, *by former experience*, " that the Courts of Wards and Liveries, and Tenures by Knights-Service, either of the King or " others, or by Knights-Service *in capite*, or Soccage " *in capite* of the King, and the conſequents upon the " ſame, have been much more burthenſome, grievous, and prejudicial," *&c.*

† See 2d and 4th Sections of the ſaid Act.

effects, provided the people be instructed in their Rights; because all such undue conditions, as I have mentioned, are absolutely *null and void* in themselves; for the law obliges us to construe them as if they had no other meaning than a *legal Grant* of lands "*in free and common so-*" *cage.*" See the 4th section of the said Act. "And be it further enacted, by "the authority aforesaid, that *all Te-*" *nures*" (there is none excepted) "here-" after to be created by the King's Ma-" jesty, his heirs, or successors, upon "*any* Gifts or Grants of *any* Manors, "Lands, Tenements, or Hereditaments, "of *any* Estate of inheritance at the "common law, shall be in *free and com-*" *mon Socage*, and *shall be adjudged* to be "in *free and common Socage onely*, and "not by Knights Service," *&c.*

SOLI DEO GLORIA ET GRATIA.

A
DECLARATION
OF THE
People's Natural Right to a Share in the Legiſlature, *&c.*

PART II.

" Qui non libere veritatem pronunciat, proditor
" eſt veritatis." 4 Inſt. Epil.

PART II.

CONTAINING

A DECLARATION

Or DEFENCE of the ſame DOCTRINE,

(*Viz.* The Natural Right of the People to a Share in the Legiſlature,)

When applied particularly

TO THE

PEOPLE of IRELAND;

In ANSWER to the ASSERTIONS of ſeveral EMINENT WRITERS on that Point, which have hitherto been permitted to paſs without due ANIMADVERSION.

WHEN the Firſt Part of this Declaration was ſent to the Preſs, I was not aware that there had been any controverſy before the ſixth of King *George* I. concerning the freedom of our fellow ſubjects in *Ireland*, or that any Engliſhman, acquainted with the principles of our excellent conſtitution of State, had ever, before that time, preſumed to advance any Doctrine, which might tend to deprive our Iriſh Brethren of their *natural freedom*, and of the ineſtimable benefits of that happy legal conſtitution, which Britiſh Subjects in general are commonly ſuppoſed to inherit by BIRTH-RIGHT!

But I have ſince had the mortification to find, that ſuch great Authorities as Lord Coke, Judge Jenkins, Lord Chief Juſtice Vaughan, Judge Blackſtone, the Honourable Mr. Juſtice Barrington, &c. might be quoted in favour of a contrary Doctrine! And as I have mentioned the Union between Great-Britain and Ireland in the Firſt Part of this Declaration, &c. as an Example of "the true conſtitutional mode of connecting Britiſh Dominions that are otherwiſe ſeparated by "nature," I thought myſelf therefore, obliged

obliged to ſearch and examine the grounds upon which theſe great and learned men have founded their opinions, that if they ſhould have *Truth* on their ſide, they might have the credit of it; but if not, that the *Truth* of this important queſtion, when plainly and impartially ſtated, might prevent for the future any ſuch undue pretenſions on the one hand, and jealouſies on the other, as have too frequently occaſioned miſunderſtandings and controverſies between the Subjects of the two Kingdoms.

Lord Huſſey, Chief Juſtice in the Reign of King *Henry* VII. ſeems to have been the Firſt who ventured publicly to aſſert, that "Statutes made in England "ſhall bind the Subject of Ireland (1):"

And

(1) "Huſſey, Chief Juſtice, diſoit que les Statuts faits "en Angleterre liera ceux de Ireland, que ne fuit moult "dedit des autres Juſtices, nient obſtant que aucun de "eux *furent en contraria opinione* le derrein term en ſon "abſence." Year Book, 1 Hen. VII. p. 3.

And though the Doctrine is unconstitutional and dangerous, if admitted in a general unlimited sense(2); yet, in justice to Judge Hussey, it must be allowed, that his Declaration was certainly right with respect to the particular case then before him,

(2) Which is clearly proved by Sir Richard Bolton, Chancellor of Ireland, in the Declaration, *&c.* printed in Harris's Hibernica, p. 29.—" As to the Opinion of " Hussy, Chief Justice, in first of Hen. 7. fol. 3. *that* " *the Statutes made in England shall bind them of Ireland,* " this Opinion, as it is put by him generally, *cannot be* " *law*; for Brooke, in abridging *that case in title Par-* " *liament,* Sect. 19. saith, that that *opinion was denied to* " *be law, the last term before*; and added further, *ta-* " *men nota, that Ireland is a Realm of itself, and hath a* " *Parliament in itself, implying thereby, that Ireland* " *could not be bound but by a Parliament of Ireland.* And " according to that, is the opinion of the Judges in " 20th Hen. VI. fol. 8. in John Pilkington's case; and " in 2d Rich. III. fol. 11. in the Merchants of Wa- " terford's case, before remembered; and likewise con- " trary to the opinion of Hussy, are the judgements of " eight several Parliaments in Ireland before the Sta- " tute of 10th of Hen. VII. viz. 13th of Edw. II. " 19th of Edw. II. 18th of Hen. VI. 29th of Hen. " VI. 32d Hen. VI. 37th Hen. VI. and 8th Edw. " IV. And since the Statute 10th Hen. VII. of five " Parliaments; viz. 28th of Hen. VIII. 33d of Hen. " VIII. 28th of Eliz. 11th of Jam. and 10th Car. " besides the Statute of 10th of Hen. VII. itself."

him, which related to the *exportation of goods from Waterford:* for, the Iriſh ſubjects themſelves do not deny the juriſdiction of Great-Britain upon the high Seas, nor in matters of external (3) commerce, though the Engliſh power, even in that reſpect, may ſometimes perhaps have been extended farther than reaſon and equity can fairly warrant. But before Lord Chief Juſtice Huſſy delivered his opinion, this proper diſtinction, concerning the Engliſh Acts binding the Iriſh *in external Tranſactions,* had been made (in his abſence) by the other Judges in a preceding

(3) This binding in external tranſactions, ſeems to be allowed (though unwillingly) by Mr. Mollyneux, (a zealous aſſerter of the liberties of Ireland in the Reign of King William.) "They ſeem" (ſays he, ſpeaking of Engliſh Acts of Parliament) "at the utmoſt reach, to extend the juriſdiction of the Engliſh "Parliament over the ſubjects of Ireland, only *in relation to their action, beyond ſeas, out of the Realm of Ireland, as they are the King of England's ſubjects,*" &c. p. 71.

a preceding term (4); which accounts for the remark of the Reporter, that this opinion

(4) " All the Judges" (but we muſt except Huſſy) " were aſſembled in the Exchequer Chamber, and " there, with reſpect to the firſt queſtion, it was ſaid, " that the lands of Ireland have a Parliament among " themſelves, and all kinds of Courts as in England; " and, by the ſame Parliament, they make laws and " change laws, and are not bound by Statutes (made) " in England, becauſe they have not here Knights of " Parliament; but this is underſtood of lands and " things only to be effected in thoſe lands, but their " perſons are ſubject to the King, and, as ſubjects, " they are bound to any thing *out of that land*, that is " done out of that land contrary to Statute, like as the " inhabitants of Calais, Gaſcoigne, Guienne, *&c.* " while they were ſubjects of the King, and in like manner are obedient under the Admiral of England concerning any thing done upon the High-Seas, and " alſo a writ of error of judgement given in Ireland " (is cognizable) in the King's Bench here in England."

Anno ſecundo Rich. III. p. 12. " Omnes Juſticiarii" (but we muſt except Huſſy) " aſſociati fuerunt " in Camera Scaccarii, et ibi quoad primam queſtionem " dicebatur, quod terræ Hiberniæ inter ſe habent " Parliamentum et omnimodo Curias prout in Anglia, " et per idem Parliamentum faciunt leges et mutant " leges, et non *obligantur per ſtatuta in Anglia, qui non* " *hic habent Milites Parliamenti*; ſed hoc intelligitur de " terris et rebus in terris ill' tantum efficiendo, ſed " perſonæ illæ ſunt ſubjectæ Regis, et *tanquam ſubjecti* " *erunt*

nion of Chief Justice Hussy "was not "much denied by the other Judges, "though some of them were of a contra- "ry opinion the last term in his absence." But, by the expression, that "*it was not* "*much denied*," it is apparent, that the other Judges did not receive the doctrine of Chief Justice Hussy, entirely and absolutely, without *some demur*; which could only consist in their adding that *due distinction* before-mentioned: for it plainly appears (notwithstanding the assertion of the Reporter) that they were not, really, of *a contrary opinion* in the former term, with respect to the case before them; which related to an *external transaction*, the same that, in their former opinion, they declared to be subject to the

 controul

"*erunt obligati* ad aliquam rem extra terram *illam fa-* "*ciendam contra Statutum*, sicut habitantes in Calesiâ, "Gascoignie, Guien, *&c.* dum fuerunt subjecti; et "similiter obedientes erunt sub Admirall' Angliæ, "de re facta super altum mare: et similiter breve de "errore de judicio reddito in Hibernia in Banco Re- "gio hic in Anglia," *&c.*

controul of England; and, therefore, there was no reafon why they fhould "*much* "*deny*" the opinion of Chief Juftice Huf-fy, fince the particular cafe before them did not require it.

But the like excufe cannot be made for Sir Edward Coke, who, in Calvin's cafe, feems to have adopted the opinion of Chief Juftice Huffy, and yet has not confidered the nature of the cafe on which the fame was delivered, having declared a fimilar opinion in an indifcriminate general fenfe (5), without paying the leaft regard to that *juft diftinction* between *the external* and *internal* Government of Ireland, which the other Judges had before fo clearly laid down and confirmed by an unanfwerable reafon (6) why the Irifh fhould

(5) "That albeit Ireland was a diftinct Dominion, "yet the title thereof being by conqueft, the fame, by "judgement of law, might by exprefs words be bound "by Act of Parliament of England." Calvin's Cafe, 7th Rep. p. 444.

(6) See the former note in p. 56. "Quia non hic ha-"bent Milites Parliamenti."

ſhould not be bound in the latter by any other laws than thoſe to which their own Parliament had aſſented, viz. "*Quia* "*non hic habent Milites Parliamenti:*" which Doctrine was agreeable alſo to what had long before been declared by that celebrated conſtitutional Lawyer, the great Judge Forteſcue on Pilkington's (7) caſe, in the 19th of Hen. VI. which was readily admitted at the ſame time by Judge Portington, and (for any thing that appears to the contrary) agreeable alſo to the opinion of all the other Judges that were then preſent; for, Sir Richard Bolton remarks, that this was not "de-"nied by Markham, Yelverton, and "Aſcough."

(7) "——et auxi la terre de Ireland eſt ſevere del' "Roiaume d' Angleterre: car ſi un diſme ou quin-"zime ſoit grante icy, ceo *ne liera ceux d'Ireland* "meſq; le Roy manderoit m cel' eſtat" (for eſtatute) "en Ireland ſoubz ſon Grand Seel, ſinon que ils veul' "en leur Parliament ceo approver mes s' ils veul al-"lower ceo, donq ſera tenu la et ils ſeront liés par "icel'." Year Book 19th Hen. VI. p. 8.

" Afcough (8)." Sir John Fortefcue had declared, that, " if a tenth or fif-" teenth

(8) The cafe is ftated by Sir Richard Bolton, Chancellor of Ireland, in his Declaration, &c. printed in Harris's Hibernica, p. 15. as follows: " That " one John Pilkington brought a fcire facias againft " one A. to fhew caufe, why Letters Patents, " whereby the King had granted an office in Ire-" land to the faid A. fhould not be repealed, whereas, " the faid John Pilkington had the fame Office grant-" ed him by former Letters Patents granted by the " fame King, to occupy to himfelf or his Deputy. " Whereupon the faid A. was warned and appeared, " and faid, ' That the *land of Ireland, time beyond the* " *memory of man, hath been a land feparated and fevered* " *from the Realm of England*, and ruled and *governed by* " *the cuftoms and laws of the fame land of Ireland*. And " that the Lords of the fame land, which are of the " King's Council, have ufed, from time to time in the " *abfence of the King, to elect a Juftice*, which Juftice, fo " elected, hath power to pardon and punifh all felo-' nies, trefpaffes, *&c. and to affemble a Parliament*; and " by the advice of the Lords and *Commonalty to make* " *Statutes*; *and he alledgeth further*, that a Parliament " was affembled, and that it was ordained by the faid " Parliament, that every man who had any office with-" in the faid land, before a certain day, *and he puts the* " *day in certain*, fhall occupy the faid Office by himfelf, " or otherwife that he fhall forfeit his office. *And* " *fheweth further*, how the faid John Pilkington oc-" cupied the faid office by a deputy, and that, info-" much as he came not in proper perfon to refide upon " his office before the day, that his office was void, " and

" teenth were granted here, this ſhould " not bind thoſe of Ireland, even though " the

" and that the King, by his Letters Patents, granted " the ſaid office, ſo become void, to the ſaid A. and " prayed that the ſaid Letters Patents ſhould be effec- " tual, and not repealed.' And upon the plea the " ſaid John Pilkington demurred in law. In the ar- " gument of which caſe, it was debated by the Judges, " Yelverton, Forteſcue, Portington, Markham, and " Aſcough, whether the ſaid preſcription were good, " or void in law; Yelverton and Portington held the " preſcription void; *but Forteſcue, Markham, and Aſ-* " *cough*, held the preſcription good, and that the *Let-* " *ters Patents made to A. were good and effectual*, and " ought not to be repealed: and in the argument of " this caſe it was agreed, by Forteſcue and Portington, " *that if a tenth or fifteenth be granted by Parliament in* " *England*, that ſhall not *bind them in Ireland*; although " the King ſend the ſame *Statute into Ireland under his* " *great ſeal: except they in Ireland will in their Parlia-* " *ment approve it*; but if they will *approve it, then it* " *ſhall bind in Ireland.* And Portington ſaid, that if a " tenth be granted in the Parliament of England, *that* " *ſhall not bind in Ireland*, becauſe they have not any " *commandment by writ to come to our Parliament*; and " this was not denied by Markham, Yelverton, or " Aſcough. Upon this caſe theſe points following are " to be obſerved, Firſt, that the Lords of the Council " of Ireland had then power, in the *abſence of the King,* " *and vacancy of a Lieutenant or Deputy, to elect a Juſtice,* " and that is plainly proved by the preamble of the " Statutes of 33d of Hen. VIII. chap. 2. in Ireland. " The words are theſe; ' For as much as continually " ſithens

"the King ſhould ſend the ſame Statute "into Ireland under his great ſeal, ex-"cept they will in their Parliament ap-"prove it; but, if they will allow it," "(*i.e.*) "then it ſhall be held there, "and

"ſithens the conqueſt of this Realm of Ireland, it "hath been uſed in this ſame Realm of Ireland, that "at every ſuch time, as it hath chaunced the ſame Realm "to be deſtitute of a Lieutenant, Deputy, Juſtice, or "other head Governour, by death, ſurrender, or de-"parture out of the ſaid Realm, or otherwiſe, the "Council of this Realm of Ireland, for the time be-"ing, have uſed, by the laws and uſages of the ſame, "to aſſemble themſelves *together to chooſe and elect a* "*Juſtice, to be Ruler and Governor of this Realm*, till "the King's Highneſs had deputed and ordained a "Lieutenant, Deputy, or other Governor for the ſame "Realm; which Juſtice, ſo being elected, was, and "hath been, always by the ancient laws and cuſtoms "of this ſaid Realm of Ireland, authoriſed to do and "exerciſe the ſaid roume of Deputy there, for the good "rule and governance, and leading of the King's ſub-"jects within the ſaid Realm of Ireland, and in mi-"niſtration of Juſtice, with divers other authorities, "pre-eminences, and juriſdictions there; which uſage, "election, and authority of the ſaid Juſtice, hath "been many times ratified and confirmed by divers "Statutes in this Realm provided and made. But this "order of election of a Juſtice is now, by the ſaid Sta-"tute of 33d of Hen. VIII. altered; as by the ſaid "Statute more at large may appear."

"and they ſhall be bound by it." And to this point Judge Portington expreſsly declared his aſſent (9), " Jeo veux bien" (ſays he) and then aſſigns the inconteſtible reaſon, " *pur ceo,*" becauſe they (the Iriſh ſubjects) " *have no ſummons* " *with us to come to Parliament.*"

But Lord Coke has unfortunately neglected to weigh the importance of this juſt *Reaſon*, and conſequently has been led to miſconſtrue the doctrine to which it has at different times been applied by the Judges; for, in Calvin's Caſe, (7th Rep. p. 447.) he cites the opinion of the Judges in 2d Rich. III. beforementioned, *viz.* " That Ireland hath a Parliament, " and they make laws, *and our Statutes* " *do not bind them:*" and he cites alſo their reaſon, *viz.* " *becauſe they do not* " *ſend*

(9) " —— et auxi quant a ceo que Forteſcue ad dit, " que ſi un Diſme ſoit grante en le Parliament icy, " *ceo ne liera ceux* d' Ireland; *Jeo veux bien pur ceo que* " *ils n'ont commandment* ove nous per breve de venir al' " Parliament." Year Book, 19th Hen. VI. p. 8.

"*ſend Knights to* (our) *Parliament*;" but he adds, in a parentheſis, that "this "is to be underſtood, *unleſs they be eſpe*-"*cially named* (10)". Thus he is ſo far from perceiving the weight of *the Reaſon* aſſigned by the former Judges, that he has ventured to ſet it aſide (as if it had no meaning at all) by the inſertion of an arbitrary parentheſis in the middle of the ſentence, without aſſigning a ſtronger *Reaſon*, or even any *Reaſon* at all for his authority; and therefore, we are certainly bound to prefer the Declaration of the other Judges, who founded their opinion on *a clear legal Reaſon*, that has never yet been diſproved; for "the REASON "*of the Law is the Life* of the Law" (11).

The

(10) "And 2d Rich. III. 12." (ſays he) "Hiber-"nia habet Parliamentum, et faciunt leges, et noſtra "Statuta non ligant eos, quia non mittunt Milites ad "Parliamentum," (which is to be underſtood unleſs they be eſpecially named) "ſed perſonæ eorum ſunt "ſubjecti Regis ſicut habitantes in Caleſia, Gaſconia, "et Guyan." &c. Calvin's Caſe, 7 Rep. p. 447.

(11) "Ratio Legis eſt anima Legis." Jenk. Cent. p. 45.

The *naming* or *not naming* Ireland, in our English Acts, cannot in the least affect the argument of the former Judges; for, if it holds good to secure the Irish subjects from being bound, *when not* "*especially named*," (which is allowed even by Sir Edward Coke himself,) it certainly is equally effectual *when they are named*; or rather, (I ought to say,) the Reason is much more forcible in the latter case, which apparently enhances the propriety and importance of it; because, when the business relating to Ireland is debated, it is manifest that the Irish subjects stand most in need of a *due representation*, which cannot therefore be denied them at such a time, without the most flagrant violation of Justice and natural Equity!

But, lest any of my Readers should still retain any doubt concerning the groundless Doctrine broached by Sir Edward

 Coke,

Coke, that English Statutes bind in Ireland when "*especially named*," I have yet another Authority to add, which must needs turn the scale, being no less than the testimony even of Sir Edward Coke himself upon this very point! Let his own words judge him.

He informs us, in his 4th Inst. cap. 76. p. 350. that "sometimes the King "of England called his Nobles of Ire- "land to *come to his Parliament of Eng- "land*," &c. and, after reciting the form of the Writ used on such occasions (12), he adds—"an excellent President" (says he) "to be followed *whensoever any Act "of Parliament shall be made in England "concerning the Statute of Ireland*," &c.

But,

(12) "10 Octobris Rex affectans pacificum "Statum terræ Hiberniæ, mandavit Richardo de Bur- "go Com. Ulton. et aliis nobilibus terræ predictæ, "quod sint ad Parliamentum suum quod summoneri "fecit apud Westm. in octabus sancti Hillarii prox. "ad tractand. ibid. cum proceribus, &c. regni sui su- "per Statu terræ prædictæ." Rot. Parl., 8. E. 2. m. 31.

But, if this be "*an excellent President*," the same spirit of justice, which inclines us to approve it as such, must needs force us to condemn *the opposite notion*, concerning mere English Statutes *binding Ireland*, when "*especially named*:" and consequently it must appear, that Lord Coke was not sufficiently upon his guard when he advanced this unjust Doctrine. And yet, alas! he has repeated the same in this very page, immediately after the Information, before quoted, concerning the Nobles of Ireland being summoned to the Parliament of England; for he adds,—" and *by special words*" (says he) " the Parliament of England *may bind* " *the Subjects of Ireland*;" &c. but, it luckily happens, that he is less reserved in this place than in the other passage already mentioned, where the same Doctrine is asserted; for here he has attempted to justify his opinion by an example, which, out of respect to so great an author, we may, of courſe, preſume to be the very beſt that could have been produced for that purpoſe; eſpecially ſince he mentions it as "*one example for* "*many*;" and yet, happily for the truth, this "*one example for many*" proves nothing ſo much (when duly conſidered) as the direct contrary to his aſſertion, about *binding Ireland* "by *ſpecial* "*words*," &c. for it amounts to an *implied acknowledgment, upon public record*, of the injuſtice of pretending to "*bind the Subjects of Ireland*" without their expreſs conſent; being, in reality, a copy of the King's Writ (before-mentioned) to ſummon the *Nobles of Ireland* "to the Parliament at Weſt-"minſter, *there* to treat with the No-"bles, *&c.* of his Kingdom *upon the* "*State of the ſaid Land*," *i. e.* Ireland. Thus it is plain that the Engliſh Legiſlature, even ſo early as in the Reign of Edward II. (by whom the Writ was iſ-

ſued,)

ſued) did not eſteem it equitable to debate " upon *the State of the ſaid Land,*"— (" ſuper ſtatu terræ prædictæ,") without ſome legiſlative repreſentation thereof: But, beſides this " *one example for* " *all,*" Sir Edward Coke has given us alſo, in the ſame page, a memorandum, from the Parliament Rolls of the 35th of Edw. III, (13) of Writs being iſſued *even to Peereſſes,* who, in their own right, held lands in Ireland, and of theſe no leſs than nine, to ſummon them to ſend Repreſentatives, or proper perſons, to confer with the Parliament; " ad mit- " tendum fide dignos ad colloquium."

And

(13) Rot. Parl. 35. E. 3. irrot. ſic. — Anno 35, E. 3. de concilio ſummonit. pro terr. habentibus in Hibernia.

Maria Comitiſſa Norf.
Ælianora Com. Orm.
Jana la Deſpencer,
Philippa Com. de la Marche,
Johanna Fitzwater,
Agnes Com. Penbroke,
Margaretta de Roos,
Matildis Com. Oxoniæ,
Catherina Com. Athol.
— ad mittendum fide dignos ad colloquium.

And consequently if Lord Coke's Doctrine (for which he has cited these examples) had, in those early times, been current, *viz.* that " by *special words* " the Parliament of England may bind " the Subjects of Ireland," it is apparent, that the same could not have been understood in any other light than that of *including* a due representation of the Irish Parliament *within* the Parliament of England; which the examples themselves sufficiently demonstrate (14): And that

(14) In the same page likewise, (4th Inst. p. 350.) Lord Coke has produced still more evidence to prove the *Parliamentary Rights of the Irish Subjects*; for he cites the Parliament rolls of 10th of Edw. II.—" De " Parliamentis *singulis annis* in Hibernia tenendis, et " de legibus, et consuetudinibus *ibidem* emendandis;" and he remarks thereupon,—" Hereby it appeareth," (says he) " that there *were* Parliaments *holden in Ireland* " before this time, and order taken at this Parliament," (says he,) " that they should be holden *every year*, and " the like Acts were made in England, in 4th E. III. " and 36th E. III. for Parliaments to be holden in " England;" so that regular *annual* Parliaments were established *in Ireland* BEFORE *they were in England!*

that this was really the caſe, is clearly proved by ſome other Engliſh records, cited by Mr. Mollyneux, in his Caſe of Ireland, pp. 73, and 74. whereby it appears, that even "Knights of the "Shires, Citizens, and Burgeſſes, were "elected in the Shires, Cities, and "Boroughs, *of Ireland*, to ſerve in Par-"liament *in England*" (15); which ancient

(15) "Formerly" (ſays Mr. Mollyneux) "when "Ireland was but thinly peopled, and the Engliſh "laws not fully current in all parts of the Kingdom, "it is probable, that then they could not frequently "aſſemble with conveniency or ſafety to make laws in "their own Parliament at home; and therefore, du-"ring the heats of rebellions, or confuſion of the "times, they were forced to enact laws in England. "But then this was always by their proper Repreſen-"tatives: For we find, that in the Reign of Edward "the Third, and by what foregoes, it is plain it *was "ſo in Edward the Firſt's time; Knights of the Shire, "Citizens, and Burgeſſes, were elected in the Shires, Ci-"ties, and Boroughs of Ireland, to ſerve in Parliament in "England*; and have ſo ſerved accordingly. For, "amongſt the records of the Tower of London, Rot. "Clauſ. 50. Edward the Third, Parl. 2. Memb. 23. "we find a writ from the King at Weſtminſter, di-"rected to James Butler, Lord Juſtice of Ireland, and "to R. Archbiſhop of Dublin, his Chancellor, re-"quiring

cient privilege of the *Irish Commons* has either been unknown, or else over-looked

" quiring them to issue writs, under the great Seal of
" Ireland, to the several Counties, Cities, and Bo-
" roughs, for satisfying the expences of the men of
" that land, who last came over to serve in Parliament
" in England. And, in another roll, the 50th of Edw.
" III. Membr. 19. on complaint to the King by John
" Draper, who was chosen Burgess of Cork by writ,
" and served in the Parliament of England, and yet
" was denied his expences by some of the Citizens,
" care was taken to reimburse him.

" If, from these last mentioned records, it be con-
" cluded that the Parliament of England may bind
" Ireland; it must also be allowed, that the people of
" Ireland ought to have their Representatives in the
" Parliament of England. And this, I believe, we
" should be willing enough to embrace; but this is an
" happiness we can hardly hope for.

" This sending of Representatives out of Ireland to
" the Parliament in England, on some occasions, was
" found in process of time to be very troublesome and
" inconvenient; and this we may presume was the
" reason that, afterwards, when times were more
" settled, we fell again into our old track and regu-
" lar course of Parliaments in our own country; and
" hereupon the laws afore-noted, page 64, were en-
" acted, establishing, that *no law made in the Parliament*
" *of England should be of force in Ireland, till it was al-*
" *lowed and published in Parliament here.*"

looked and forgot by Lord Coke; and indeed it is not probable that the Irish Parliament was ever summoned to England *regularly*, or as a matter *of course*, to meet the English Parliament, but only on extraordinary occasions, wherein the Subjects of Ireland were particularly concerned, and could not, we may presume, be "*specially named*" and bound, (that is consistently with *natural equity* and their own *just rights*) without their express assent: for it is apparent that *regular Parliaments* were held *in Ireland*, both BEFORE, *since*, and even *during the Reigns of those very Princes* who issued writs to summon them to *England*; which latter, therefore, can only be attributed to some extraordinary or peculiar circumstances, (out of common course) which rendered it necessary.

In addition to the clear Precedents before cited, it may not perhaps be improper to take notice of a circumstance quoted by the Honourable Mr. Juſtice Barrington, from Petyt, MSS. Vol. XXVII. p. 294. for though it is not a Precedent exactly to the point in queſtion, (*i. e.* the ſending Repreſentatives from Ireland to the *Engliſh Parliament,)* yet it tends to corroborate the ſame equitable Doctrine concerning the neceſſity of *Repreſentation* in general, which ought to be the baſis of all determinations either in the *Privy Council,* (to which the example particularly relates,) or elſewhere. " There is a writ (ſays he) of " Edward III. in the 50th Year of his " Reign, to oblige the Inhabitants of " *Cork* to pay the expences of *John* " *Droup*, who is ſtated to have *been cho-* " *ſen by the Community to attend the King's* " *Privy Council in England*(16)." The Buſineſs of his attendance, however, does not appear; but on whatever account he might attend *the Privy Council,* he was probably

(16) " Obſervations on the more ancient Statutes," &c. p. 145.

probably the ſame perſon that is mentioned in the record before cited from Mr. Mollyneux, by the name of *John Draper*, "who was choſen Burgeſs of "*Cork* by Writ, and ſerved in the Par-"liament of England;" for, as the other circumſtances correſpond, both with reſpect to *the place* from whence he came, and *the year* of his being ſent, it is natural to conclude, that the ſmall diſagreement in the name may have been occaſioned by ſome accidental miſtake, *viz. John Droup* for *John Draper*, or *vice verſa*; and he might ſerve the Inhabitants of *Cork* in the double capacity of *Repreſentative in Parliament*, and Agent for them to the *Privy Council*; or perhaps his ſummons and attendance, even at the *King's Privy Council*, might have been in his *parliamentary* capacity; for if a due Repreſentation from Ireland was to attend the King here *in his Privy Council*, ſuch an Aſſembly might, without danger, I apprehend, be allowed all the powers of an *effectual Legislature to bind Ireland*, provided the respective branches of Irish Representation be preserved entire and distinct; for the *English Privy Council* could have no legal voice in such a case, except that of advising the assent or dissent of the Sovereign; and yet, whenever it was necessary to call *a distinct* Irish Parliament in England, it is not improbable, but that they might be summoned to meet the *King in his Privy Council* by way of distinguishing their separate Assembly from the joint-meeting of the English and Irish Parliaments before-mentioned. And that such *distinct Irish Parliaments* have sometimes been held *in England* appears by a record cited by Mr. Mollyneux (17), wherein mention is made of Statutes

(17) " There have been other Statutes or Ordinances, made in England for Ireland, which may *reasonably* be of force here, because they were made " and

Statutes made at *Lincoln* and at *York* in the 9th of Edw. I. by the *exprefs affent of the Irifh Parliament in all its branches of Legiflature*, (viz. per nos de affenfu Prelatorum, Comitorum et Communitates *Regni noftri Hiberniæ)* without the leaft mention of *the Englifh Parliament*. Thus it appears probable, that the Irifh have been *reprefented* in England, as well

" and *affented to by our own Reprefentatives*. Thus " we find in the White Book of the Exchequer in " Dublin, in the 9th Year of Edward the Firft, a writ " fent to his Chancellor of Ireland, wherein he men- " tions *Quædam Statuta per nos de Affenfu Prelatorum* " *Comitum Baronum & Communitates Regni noftri Hiber-* " *niæ, nuper apud Lincoln & quædam alia Statuta poft-* " *modum apud Eborum facta*. Thefe we may fuppofe " were either Statutes made at the requeft of the States " of Ireland, to explain to them the Common Law of " England; or if they were introductive of new laws, " yet they might well be of force in Ireland, being " enacted by the affent of our own Reprefentatives, " the Lords Spiritual and Temporal, and Commons " of Ireland; as the words afore-mentioned do fhew: " and, indeed, thefe are inftances fo far from making " againft our claim, that I think nothing can be more " plainly for us; for it manifeftly fhews, that the " King and Parliament of England would not enact " laws, to bind Ireland, without the concurrence of the " Reprefentatives of this Kingdom."

well in *ſeparate* as in *joint* Parliaments; and, upon ſuch equitable terms of Repreſentation *in England*, I preſume, no Iriſh Patriot will object to the *binding* of *Engliſh* Statutes (18) whether Ireland be "*eſpecially named*" or not; becauſe the juſt reaſon of objection, before cited from the Judges in the 19th of Henry VI. and 2d Richard III. no longer ſubſiſts when a due Repreſentation is allowed.

How

(18) —— "Add hereunto," (ſays Sir William Petty in his Political Survey of Ireland, p. 31.) "that "if both Kingdoms were *under one Legiſlative Power* "*and Parliament, the Members whereof ſhould be pro*"*portionable in power and wealth of each Nation*, there "would be no danger ſuch a Parliament ſhould do any "thing to the prejudice of the *Engliſh* intereſt in *Ire*"*land*; nor could the *Iriſh* ever complain of partiality "when they ſhall be *freely and proportionably repreſented* "in all Legiſlatures." The ſame author has alſo made a very ſtriking remark in p. 97, concerning the neceſſity of maintaining the independence of the *Legiſlative Power*, whether we apply the ſame to *Ireland*, or to any other part of the *Britiſh* Empire; for "why ſhould "men" (ſays he) "endeavour to get eſtates, where "*the Legiſlative Power* is not agreed upon, and where "tricks and words deſtroy *natural Rights* and Pro"perty?"

How much *later* than the Reign of Edw. III. this practice was continued, of *occasionally* ſummoning the Iriſh Parliament *into England*, does not appear; though we may be certain that it did not continue ſo late as the Reign of Hen. VI. becauſe the great Forteſcue and the other Judges, his cotemporaries, could not have declared (as has already been ſhewn) that " a tenth or fifteenth, granted " *here*, ſhould *not bind* thoſe of Ireland," if the practice of ſending *Repreſentatives from thence* had continued to that time: nevertheleſs, the proofs already produced are amply ſufficient to confute the obſervation of Judge Jenkins in his 4th Century, p. 164, *viz.* that " the Statutes of England, which *expreſsly* name " *Ireland, bind them and their Lands and* " *Goods.* As the Statute of York" (ſays he) " made 12th E. II. and the 13th " E. I. de Mercatoribus, and others:" For, as I have produced ſufficient examples

ples of the Irish Parliament being summoned to England in *both the Reigns* which he has mentioned, these Statutes cited by him can afford no testimony of what he supposes, because the Irish might probably have been *represented in those very* Parliaments; for which opinion (I have already shewn) there is *some evidence*, and I am not apprehensive that *any evidence at all* can be produced to the contrary.

The same reply holds good also, against the most material examples cited in Serjeant Mayart's answer to Sir Richard Bolton's Declaration (19), setting forth

(19) The learned Editor of these two Tracts, (Mr. Harris,) who has published them in his Hibernica, (printed at Dublin in 1770,) supposes, that *Sir Richard Bolton* was *not* the author of this Declaration, and informs us, in his Preface, that he is "inclined rather to give the honour of the performauce to Patrick "Darcey, Esq; an eminent Lawyer and an active "Member of the House of Commons in the Parliament assembled at Dublin in 1640," who was the author

forth " how, and by what means the " Laws and Statutes *of England* from

M

" time

thor of a ſimilar argument delivered by him at a conference with a Committee of the Iriſh Lords in 1641, (printed in 1643.) " The conformity" (ſays Mr. Harris) " between what is alledged in the Declara-" tion, and in Darcy's Arguments, inclines me to think " him the author of that paper." But a conformity in ſubſtance between two authors, upon one and the ſame *national* queſtion, is very far from affording ſo ſubſtantial a proof of the real author as the name of *Sir Richard Bolton* upon one of the manuſcripts: Probably the impeachment of Sir Richard Bolton (in the ſame year) of High-Treaſon, for betraying (in his capacity of Chancellor of Ireland) the Conſtitution of that country †, might be another reaſon for Mr. Harris's ſuppoſition; but this very contrary behaviour, with which Sir Richard Bolton was charged, does not appear to have been ſo much the effect of his private opinion, as of his political *time-ſerving*, or yielding, with his brethren in Adminiſtration, to the arbitrary notions of Lord Strafford, the (then) Lord Lieutenant of Ireland; or perhaps the dangerous increaſing power of the papiſts at that time might occaſion his thus yielding to mea-

ſures

† Viz. For having " traiterouſly contrived, introduced, and ex-" erciſed an arbitrary and tyrannical Government, againſt Law, " throughout this Kingdom, (Ireland,) by the countenance, and aſ-" ſiſtance, of *Thomas* Earl of *Strafford*, then Chief Governor of this " Kingdom." See the 1ſt Article of Impeachment againſt Sir Richard Bolton and others, with the Speech of Mr. Audley Mervin on that occaſion, taken from Nalſon's Collection of Papers, and re-printed at Dublin in 1764, at the end of Darcy's Argument.

" time to time came to be of force *in* " *Ireland*;" and it is undeniable, that the

ſures which were ſo diametrically oppoſite to his own juſt principles ; though indeed no danger whatever can juſtify ſuch conduct, ſince " honeſty is always" (moſt certainly) " the beſt policy." Nevertheleſs, not only Serjeant Mayart's anſwer acknowledges Sir Richard as the author of the Declaration ; but Mr. Mollyneux in p. 48, and 49, cites a marginal note of Sir Richard's, (when he was Lord Chief Baron of the Exchequer in Ireland,) which he had affixed in his Edition of the Iriſh Statutes, Stat. 10 Henry VII. c. 22. to the following purport ; *reſembling* the ſubſtance of the Declaration, attributed to Sir Rich. Bolton, *much more* than the argument of Mr. Darcy, *viz.* " That in the " 13th of Edward the Second, by Parliament in this " Realm of Ireland, the Statutes of Merton, made the " 20th of Henry the Second, *and the Statutes of* Mal-" bridge, *made the* 52*d of* Henry *the Third* ; *the Statute* " *of* Weſtminſter *the firſt, made the* 3*d of* Edward *the* " *Firſt* ; *the Statute of* Glouceſter, *made the* 6*th of* Ed-" ward *the Firſt* ; *and the Statute of* Weſtminſter *the ſe-" cond, made the* 13*th of* Edward *the Firſt, were all con-" firmed* in this Kingdom, (Ireland ;) *and all other Sta-" tutes which were of force in* England *were referred to* " *be examined in the next Parliament* ; *and ſo many as were* " *then allowed and publiſhed, to ſtand likewiſe for Laws* " *in this Kingdom. And in the* 10*th of* Henry *the Fourth,* " *it was enacted in this Kingdom of* Ireland, That the " Statutes made in *England* ſhould not be of force in " this Kingdom, unleſs they were allowed and pub-" liſhed in this Kingdom by Parliament. *And the like* " *Statute* the *Irish* Parliament have in general thought it neceſſary to examine, and to authenticate by the *expreſs aſſent* of their own aſſemblies, ſuch *Engliſh* Statutes as they judged proper to be admitted as Law within their own Iſland; of which Sir Richard Bolton has produced a great variety of examples (20), ſome *general*, and

" *Statute was made again in the 29th of* Henry *the Sixth.* " *Theſe Statutes are not to be found in the* Rolls, nor any " Parliament *Roll of that time: but he* (Sir Richard " Bolton) *had ſeen the ſame exemplified under the great* " *Seal, and the* exemplification *remaineth in the Treaſury* " *of the* city of Waterford." Mollyneux's Caſe of Ireland, pp. 48 & 49.

(20) " But ſuch Statutes, as have been made in " England ſince the 11th of King John, *and are intro-* " *ductory and poſitive, making new Laws, or any ways* " *altering, adding unto, or diminiſhing the ancient Com-* " *mon Laws,* have not been binding or any ways of " force in Ireland, until ſuch time as they have been " enacted, allowed, and approved of, by Act of Par- " liament in Ireland; as may appear by the judge- " ments of nine Parliaments holden *there,* viz. *in the* " *13th of Edward* II. in a Parliament in Ireland, the " Statutes of Merton and Marlebridge, made in the " time of Henry III. and the Statutes of Weſtminſter " 1ſt, and of Weſtminſter 2d, and the Statute of " Glouceſter, made in the time of Edward I. were " confirmed

and ſome *particular*, made at different periods of time, from the 13th of Edward

" confirmed and approved to be of force in Ireland; " and all other Statutes, which were of force in Eng- " land, were then referred to be examined *in the next* " *Parliament, and ſo many of them, as ſhould be then al-* " *lowed, and publiſhed, to be accepted for Laws in Ireland.* " And afterwards, in a Parliament holden in Ireland " in 19th of Edward II. it was enacted that *the Sta-* " *tutes made in England ſhould not be of force in the King-* " *dom of Ireland, unleſs they were allowed and publiſhed* " *in that Kingdom by Parliament*; and the like Statute " *was made again in 29th of Henry* VI.—But theſe Sta- " tutes are not to be found in theſe parliament rolls, " nor any parliament rolls at that time, but the *ſame are* " *exemplified under the great Seal, and the exemplifications* " *were remaining in the Treaſury of the city of Waterford.* " And it is moſt certain, that not only theſe parlia- " ment rolls, but alſo many other rolls and records " miſcarried in thoſe troubleſome and diſtempered " times, which have been in Ireland: For in all the " times of Edw. III.—Rich. II.—Hen. IV.—and " Hen. V. which is almoſt an hundred years, there is " not any parliament roll to be found; and yet it is " moſt certain, that divers Parliaments were holden in " thoſe times. Moreover in 28th of Edw. I.—5th of " Edw. III.—14th of Edw. III.—25th of Edw. III. " —34th of Edw. III.—and 7th of Rich. II. divers " good laws were made in England by ſeveral Acts of " Parliament againſt the extortions and oppreſſions of " Purveyors; which laws were never received, nor " put into execution in Ireland, untill the 18th of

" Hen.

ward II. to the Reign of King Charles I. the time when he wrote, and of these examples

" Hen. VI. chap. I. that it was enacted, agreed, and " established by Parliament in Ireland, that all Sta- " tutes made against Purveyors within the Realm of " England should be holden and kept in all points, and " put in execution in Ireland. ——— Afterwards in " the time of Edward IV. a doubt was conceived, " whether the Statute made in England in 6th of Rich. " II. chap. 5. concerning Rape, ought to be of force " in Ireland, without a confirmation thereof by Par- " liament: for the clearing of which ambiguity and " doubt, in 8th Edward IV. chap. 1. in Ireland, it was " enacted, by authority of Parliament, that *the said* " *Statute of 6th of Richard* II. *be adjudged and proved in* " *force and strength*; and that the Statute may be of " force in this land of Ireland from the 6th day of " March then last past, and from thenceforth the said " Act, and all other Statutes and Acts made by the au- " thority of the said Parliament, within the Realm of " England, be ratified and confirmed, and adjudged " by the authority of Parliament, in their *force and* " *strength from the said 6th Day of March.*" ——— So " as until the said Statute of 8th Edw. IV.—the said " Statute of 6th Rich. II. was not wholly of force in " Ireland; and that may appear by the words of the " said Statute of the 8th of Edward IV.—For by the " words thereof the said Statute of 6th Rich. II. was " to be of force *from the 6th of March then last past*, " whereas, the said Statute of 6th *Rich.* II. *had been* " *but a declaration or explanation of the Statute of Westmin-* " *ster* 2. *chap.* 34. it would have *been of force at all times*

" *since*

examples not leſs in number than eighteen, which ſurely are ſufficient to prove the uniform

" *ſince the making* of the Statute of Weſtminſter 2d. which " was in 13th Edw. I. ——— But afterwards, 10th " Hen. VII. c. 22. it was enacted in a Parliament in " Ireland," (this is one of the Acts commonly called Poining's Acts,) " that all Statutes then lately made " within the ſaid *Realm of England, concerning or belong-* " *ing to the common or public weale of the ſame, from thence-* " *forth* ſhould be deemed good and effectual in the " law, and over that accepted, uſed, and executed " within the land of Ireland at all times requiſite, ac- " cording *to the tenor and effect of the ſame; and over that* " *by the authority aforeſaid, that they, and every of them,* " *be authoriſed, proved, and confirmed in the ſaid land of* " *Ireland.*

" By all which Statutes, made from time to time in " Ireland, it plainly appeareth, *that all Statutes made in* " *England before* 10*th Hen.* VII. *concerning or belonging to* " *the public and commonwealth of England,* are made to be " of force, *and to become laws in Ireland.* ——— In " 21ſt Hen. VIII. chap. 7. an Act was made in Eng- " land, that makes it felony in a ſervant that runneth " away with the goods of his maſter or miſtreſs; and " this Act was not received in Ireland until *the ſame* " *was enacted by a Parliament holden in Ireland* in 33d " Hen. VIII. Seſſ. 1. chap. 5.—In 21ſt Hen. VIII. " chap. 19.—There was a law made in England, that " all Lords might diſtrain upon the lands of them " holden for their rents and ſervices, and to make their " avowries, not naming the tenant, but upon the " lands:

uniform ſenſe of the *Iriſh* Parliament upon this point in every age ſince they received the *Engliſh* Law.

Of

" lands: but this law was not received in Ireland un- " til it was enacted there in 33d Hen. VIII. Seſſ. 1. " chap. 7.—An Act was made in England in Anno 31. " Hen. VIII. chap. 1. that joint tenants, and te- " nants in common, ſhould be compelled to make par- " tition; which Act was not received in Ireland until " it was enacted there in 33d Hen. VIII. Seſſ. 1. chap. " 10.—In 27th Hen. VIII. chap. 10. the Statute of " Uſes was made in England, for transferring of Uſes " into poſſeſſion; which Statute was never received, " nor of force in Ireland, till the ſame was enacted in " Ireland, 10th Car. 1. chap. 1.—So likewiſe, 32d " Hen. VIII. chap. 1. a Statute was enacted in Eng- " land, whereby it is directed, how lands and tene- " ments may be diſpoſed by will, and concerning ward- " ſhip, and primer ſeizins; which Statute was never " received, nor of force in Ireland, until it was en- " acted by Parliament in Ireland, in 10th Car. I. chap. " 2.—In Anno 1ſt Eliz. chap. 5. there was an Act " made in England for the uniformity of the Com- " mon-Prayer, and Adminiſtration of the Sacraments; " which Act was not received in Ireland, until the ſame " was confirmed and eſtabliſhed by Parliament in Anno " 2d Eliz. c. 2.—In Anno 5th Eliz. c. 9. there was an " Act of Parliament made in England for the puniſh- " ment of wilful perjury; which Act was not of force " in Ireland until the ſame was enacted by a Parlia- " ment in Ireland, in 28th Eliz. chap. 1.—Another " Act was made in England in Anno 3d Eliz. chap. 12.

" for

Of the general examples which he has cited, that in the 10th of Hen. VII. (one of Poining's Acts) whereby all the English

" for the punishment of witchcraft and sorcery, and " another Act in the same year, chap. 14. for the pu- " nishment of forgery; which Acts were not of force " in Ireland until the same were enacted by Parlia- " ment there in 28th Eliz. chap. 2, 3.——In 28th " Hen. VIII. chap. 15. there was an Act made in " England for the punishment of piracy; which Act " was not of force in Ireland until the same was en- " acted in Ireland in 12th of James, chap. 2.——In " 27th of Eliz. chap. 4. an Act was made in Eng- " land against fraudulent conveyances, which Act was " not of force, nor received in Ireland, until the same " was enacted in Ireland, 10th Car. I. chap. 3.—— " Besides many other Acts made in the several reigns " of Henry VIII.—Edward VI.—Queen Elizabeth,— " King James,—and the King's Majesty who now is. " ——In 24th Hen. VIII. chap. 12. &c. an Act " was made in England concerning appeals made to " Rome, which Act doth *by express words extend to* " *all his Majesty's dominions*; yet the same *was not* " *received*, nor of force *in Ireland*, until it was enacted " by Act of Parliament *there* in 28th Hen. VIII. chap. " 6.——Also the Statute of 28th Hen. VIII. chap. 8. " made in England concerning the first-fruits of the " Clergy, extended by express words to any of the " King's dominions; yet the same was not received, " or of force in Ireland, until it was enacted there by " Parliament in 28th Hen. VIII. chap. 8.——Likewise " the

Engliſh Statutes then in force were adopted by the Iriſh, is the moſt remarkable; and it is neceſſary to take particular notice of this Act, becauſe the effect of it is frequently miſunderſtood; for ſome have ſuppoſed, that hereby "all "the Statutes, made in the Parliament of "England concerning the public, ſhould "be obſerved in Ireland," without obſerving any farther diſtinction (21); as if

N they

" the Act of faculties made in England 25th Hen. "VIII. chap. 21. extended *by expreſs words to all* "*the King's dominions*; yet the ſame *was not re-* "*ceived*, or of force, *in Ireland*, until it was enacted "by Parliament in Ireland, 28th Henry VIII. "chap. 19."

(21) In this indiſcriminate manner Monſieur Rapin has expreſſed himſelf, and has thereby given a wrong Idea of the Iriſh Legiſlature to ſuch of his readers as do not care for the trouble of ſeeking better information; for, in ſpeaking of the two Statutes, commonly called *Poining's Acts*, (after having mentioned that Act relating to the King's permiſſion for aſſembling the Parliament,) he adds, " Un autre portoit que tous les " Actes faits dans le Parliament d'Angleterre, con- " cernant le Public, ſeroient obſervéz en Irlande. Ces " deux Statuts ſont encore en force aujourdui." Tome 4. p. 469.

they thought the Statute capable of including, not only all the English Acts then made, but, likewise, all such as should be ordained in future: and, if this had really been the case, it would have been in vain to have contended for the Liberties of Ireland; but the Act itself is not capable of such a *construction*, notwithstanding that some have thought it doubtfully worded. The tenor of it is recited by Lord Coke, in his 4th instit. p. 351. as follows: " That all Statutes, *late* " made within the Realm of *England*, " concerning or belonging to the com- " mon or public weal of the same, from " henceforth be deemed good and effec- " tual in the Law, and over that be ac- " cepted, used, and executed, within " this land of *Ireland*, in all points, *&c.*" And though the word *late* was afterwards deemed a doubtful expression, with respect to the extent of its effect, yet it sufficiently restrains the Act to the introduction

tion of ſuch *Engliſh* Statutes *only* as were of prior date; which effect is confirmed alſo by a reſolution of the Judges, in the 10th of James, cited by Lord Coke in the ſame page (22); and he has likewiſe ſtated the true effect of that Act in his 1ſt Inſtitute, 141 *b*. *Viz.*

" By an Act of Parliament (called " *Poining's Law*), holden in Ireland" (ſays he) " in the 10th yeare of Henry the 7th, it is enacted, That all Statutes, made in this Realme of *England* BEFORE THAT TIME, ſhould be " of

(22) " And, Hil. 10. Jacobi Regis, it was reſolved, by the two Chief Juſtices and Chief Baron, that this word, (*late*,) in the beginning of this act, had the ſenſe of (*before*), ſo that this Act extended to *Magna Carta*, and to *all* Acts of Parliament made in England *before* this Act of 10. H. 7. But it is to be obſerved, that ſuch Acts of Parliament as have been made in England ſince 10. H. 7. wherein Ireland is not particularly named or generally included, extend not thereunto; for that, albeit it be governed by the ſame law, yet is it *a diſtinct Realm* or *Kingdome*, and (as hath been ſaid) *hath Parliaments there*." 4. Inſt. p. 351.

" of force, and be put in use, within " the Realme of *Ireland*," &c.

This Act of Poining's, therefore, sufficiently proves what Sir Richard Bolton intended by citing it, *viz.* that the *Irish* did not esteem the *English* Laws *binding in that Kingdom* until allowed by the Authority of their own Parliament, otherwise the Act itself had been nugatory, as also the other Irish Acts which he has cited for the same purpose; in some of which, it seems, the Parliament itself expressly asserted the Doctrine for which he contends; as in that of the 19th of Edw. II. wherein it was enacted, " That " the Statutes, made in *England*, SHOULD " NOT BE OF FORCE in the Kingdom of " *Ireland*, unless they were allowed and " published in that Kingdom by Parlia- " ment." (23) Sir Richard Bolton also informs

(23) See Sir Richard Bolton's Declarations, &c. in Harris's Hibernica, p. 15.

informs us, that "a like Statute was "made again in the 29th of Henry VI." and therefore, notwithſtanding that Serjeant Mayart has taken great pains, and filled many pages with citations of precedents from old Records of Law Caſes, Writs, &c. (in order to prove that *Engliſh* Acts of Parliament have been referred to, and allowed in judicial Proceedings, before the ſame were confirmed in *Ireland*,) yet all his labour has been beſtowed in vain; for (beſides that he ought firſt to have proved the Acts in queſtion to have been made by the *Engliſh* Parliament alone, without any ſuch repreſentation of the *Iriſh* Parliament jointly therewith, as I have already ſhewn to have been frequently practiſed in thoſe early days) let it be alſo remarked, that, though we ſhould allow that the *Iriſh* Courts of Juſtice might, perhaps, in ſome particular caſes of *difference* between individuals, but of *indifference*

rence to the general Liberties of *Ireland*, have followed the directions of ſome mere *Engliſh* Acts of Parliament, as eſteeming them wholeſome regulations of Juſtice, proper to be adopted for the determination of the Caſes before them, yet the *Confirmation* of ſuch Acts afterwards, at different periods, clearly proves the irregularity of ſuch premature proceedings in the Courts, and that the higheſt Court of that Kingdom, the Court of Parliament, did not eſteem the *Engliſh* Acts *of ſufficient legal Authority* till confirmed by themſelves; for, otherwiſe, the *Confirmation* would have been *unneceſſary*, ſince the Acts (if Serjeant Mayart's examples are admitted) were already received into uſe; and, therefore, all ſuch Court-Precedents, as are cited by the learned Serjeant, are clearly Precedents of *Irregularities* and not of *Law*; ſo that they are not intitled to any conſideration at all; eſpecially as the Iriſh Legiſla-

ture

ture itſelf (which has certainly a better right to determine what ſhall be eſteemed Law in Ireland than any of the inferior Courts) has poſitively declared, by the expreſs Acts of the 19th of Edward II. and the 29th of Henry VI. before cited, that *Engliſh* Statutes ſhall not be of force in *Ireland*, unleſs allowed by the *Iriſh* Parliament! And agreeable to this is the Declaration of the Iriſh Houſe of Commons in 1641, Article the firſt: That "the Subjects of this his Majeſty's Kingdom of Ireland are a free people, and "to be governed only according to the "*common Law* of *England*, and Statutes "made and eſtabliſhed by Parliament in "this Kingdome of *Ireland*, and according to the lawful Cuſtomes uſed in "the ſame." p. 133.

Now, though the Conviction by theſe weighty Authorities will probably deſtroy the credit of Serjeant Mayart, as a writer,

ter, in the opinion of every honest Irish-man, yet the Irish are more obliged to this Author than he himself, perhaps, intended they should be; for he clearly proves that *a Charter of Liberties* (24), agreeing in all the Chapters with our *Magna Charta*, was *separately granted to the*

(24) " For the only mistake of *Lord Coke* is, that " he conceived" (says he) " that *Magna Charta* was " not of force in *Ireland* 'till the 10th of Hen. 7; " which is only a mistake of a matter of fact; for *in* " *truth we find*" (continues the Serjeant) " that sta-" tute was given to them of Ireland in the first year " of Hen. 3. and all the Chapters thereof (except " three or four of the last Chapters) are entered in the " Red Book of the Exchequer of Ireland, where, in " the beginning, after the King's stile recited, he " saith, Imprimis concessimus Deo, et hac præsenti " Chartâ nostrâ confirmamus pro nobis & hæredibus " nostris in perpetuum, quod Hibernica Ecclesia libera " sit, *&c.* —— First, we have granted to God, and, " by this our Charter, confirm, for us and our heirs " for ever, that the Church of Ireland be free. —— " Sir John Davis cites a Record in the Tower, 1st of " Hen. 3. Memb. 13. *of the like Charter of Liberties* " *granted* by Hen. 3. *to his Subjects in Ireland, as him-* " *self and his Father had granted to the Subjects of Eng-* " *land*; but yet this mistake is only for that Coke was " not *informed of that matter of fact.*" Harris's Hibernica, pp. 226, 227.

the King's Subjects of Ireland, without distinction, in the first year of King Henry III. so that *all the Subjects of Ireland*, (the conquered Irish not excepted,) from that very early period, and even sooner (25), were as much entitled to *English* Liberty,

O

(25) For, the *English Settlers* carried their Rights with them, and the native Irish *gladly accepted* the *English* Common Law, as soon as it was tendered to them by the *English* Conquerors, of which I have produced ample testimony in a Note on page 108. so that their just title to *English Liberty* and all the legal Immunities of the Conquerors was clearly established and confirmed by *this Irish Magna Charta.* —— They were very soon afterwards, indeed, wickedly excluded from these equitable Privileges by the inconsiderate English Settlers; many of whom, for the sake of tyrannizing over their poor neighbours, even *degenerated* (as Sir John Davies informs us in p. 32.) into the lawless Irish manners themselves, adopting the old *Irish* oppressions of Tanistry, Cosherings, Cuttings, Sessings, Coigne and Livery, *&c.* under which most wicked* pretences they devoured

* These *most wicked oppressions* originally sprang from the undue Power and unlimited Sway of the antient Irish Chieftains, or Lords, over their poor brethren; but I must refer my Readers, for a particular description of them, to Sir John Davies, who has amply set forth the gross injustice and pernicious effects of such *unlimited power* in men: nevertheless I am tempted to cite, by way of sample, what he has mentioned in one place concerning the wickedness of *Coigne* and *Livery*

Liberty, and all the Immunities and Benefits of the *English* Common Law, as the Inhabitants of England themselves: and yet Lord Coke himself, it seems (26), was not aware of this Circumstance, but "Conceived"

devoured the *poor Natives* as well as the poorer sort of *English* Settlers, and thereby occasioned almost continual Wars for several ages; which, in the end, turned out to their own great peril and disadvantage, according to the never-failing maxim, or rather warning, of the Apostle Paul; "*If ye bite and devour one another,* "take heed that ye be not *consumed one of another.*" Gal. v. 15. But, though the *Irish* were, by this wretched Policy of the *English*, long deprived of the *Benefit* of the *English* Common Law, yet this by no means deprived them of their just *Right* or *Claim* to it, which must necessarily be acknowledged to have been due from the time that the English first settled in that Country.

(26) 2d Inst. p. 2.

Livery in particular: for, in shewing the ill effects of English Degeneracy, he remarks in p. 33. "By this" (says he) "it appeareth why "the extortion of *Coigne* and *Livery* is called, in the old Statutes of "Ireland, A DAMNABLE CUSTOME, and the imposing and taking "thereof made *High-Treason*. And it is said, in an antient Discourse" (says he) "*of the Decay of Ireland,* that, though it were first invent-"ed in *Hell*, yet, if it had been used and practised there as it hath "been in Ireland, it had long since destroyed the very Kingdom of "Beelzebub." The same bad effects are produced, in some degree, by every kind of *Vassalage*; so that the bad Policy of establishing *Seigneuries* in Canada, or elsewhere, is but too apparent.

"Conceived" (ſays Serjeant Mayart, p. 226.) "that *Magna Charta* was not of "force *in Ireland* till the 10th of Hen. 7. "which is only a miſtake" (ſays he) "of "a matter of fact; for *in truth we find*" (ſays he) "that Statute was given to "them of Ireland in the firſt year of "Hen. 3. *&c.*" But though this was only "*a miſtake of a matter of fact,*" yet it was ſuch a miſtake as might probably, in great meaſure, have occaſioned the erroneous opinions ever after, of that great and worthy man, concerning the Conſtitution of Ireland.

But Serjeant Mayart has not profited ſo much as might have been expected by this knowledge that the Subjects of *Ireland* were honoured with a diſtinct Charter; for, after pointing out (in page 227) the ſeveral Chapters of the Charter, wherein (as he ſuppoſes) "that Law dif-"fers from the antient common Law,"

 he

he adds them triumphantly to his Collection of Precedents for binding *Ireland* by Statutes made in *England*; as if *a Charter of Liberties*, freely given and gladly accepted, could afford any Evidence *againſt Liberty!* For this undiſtinguiſhing man did not conſider that the King, by this Charter of Liberties, *binds and reſtrains* himſelf (rather than his People) in all the moſt dangerous points of Prerogative, wherein the Rulers of other Countries are left too much *unlimited*; and therefore that the Subjects of *Ireland* might accept the ſame (which they moſt willingly did) without the leaſt Derogation from their juſt and natural Rights.

And, as this Charter was granted to the "*King's Subjects in Ireland*" without diſtinction, it affords the moſt ample proof that even the *conquered Iriſh* were entitled to all the Immunities, Protection, and Benefits, which the *Engliſh Conquerors*

Conquerors themselves enjoyed by it: for even Serjeant Mayart himself proves (in p. 67.) that the English Laws "*were* "*given at first*" — "*tam* ANGLIS "QUAM HIBERNICIS, *as well to* ENG-"LISH AS IRISH" (27). The Irish Nation

(27) Serjeant Mayart also informs us, "That the "whole Realm of Ireland was antiently reduced into "Counties, and that the English Laws had passage "throughout the same, as appears" (says he) "by "several Pipe-Rolls of the Time of Hen. 3. in the "Exchequer of Ireland, where there are accounts" (says he) "made for fines, paid by the mere *Irish*, for *Dis*-"*seisins*, and many other kinds of Trespasses, com-"mitted by them in those places, which the Author "calls *Irish* Territories; though some of the Irish, "with their posterity after them, being always *averse* "to the English Laws, could not digest them, but hid "themselves in the bogs, mountains, *&c.*" But this aversion of "*some of the Irish*" to the English Laws is easily accounted for, since it appears very clearly, from Sir John Davies's Book, that the Irishry had much more experience and woful knowledge of *English Oppression* than of the *English Laws*; for, when any of them were driven from their Lands and Possessions through the avarice, and by the unlawful power, of the great English Lords, who found their interest in treating them as enemies, it was very *natural* for them to attempt to *disseize*, and recover their former Rights and Possessions;

tion are alſo obliged to Serjeant Mayart for ſome other Proofs in their favour, *which he intended againſt them*: for, amongſt his Precedents of *giving Law*, he informs us, in p. 219. "that, in the "Reign of King Henry II. *the common* "*Law* and *lawful* Cuſtoms of *England* "were received, planted, and eſtabliſh- "ed, in this his Majeſty's Kingdom of "Ireland;" a Point which every Iriſh Patriot is zealous to maintain! And he has favoured us, in page 220, with another notable Example of binding the *Iriſh* by *Engliſh* Laws: this, it ſeems, was in the Reign of King John, "of "whom," (ſays he triumphantly,) "in "that

Poſſeſſions: and again, when they found no Protection from the Engliſh Laws, nor other exertion thereof than that of *fining* and *puniſhing* them for ſuch "*Diſſeizins*," *&c.* which were mere *Re-entries*, it was *equally natural* for them to imbibe prejudices againſt the Engliſh Laws, and to fly to their Bogs, *&c.* Thus the *Engliſh Oppreſſions* were apparently the cauſe why *ſome* of the Iriſh were averſe to the *Engliſh Laws*; which I have expreſſed more at large in a Note on p. 108.

" that respect, it may be well said, that, " *Statuit et præcepit Leges*; he *appointed* " *and established the Laws*; as also because " he put them in writing, and left them " in his Court of Exchequer for their " better directions." but he happily informs us at the same time, (which spoils his own application of the Precedent,) that all this was done " *at the instance*" (says he) " *of the Irish*, (as the Record " saith,) or of the English who account" ed themselves Irish," &c. And therefore, as these English Laws and Customs are clearly acknowledged by himself to have been introduced " *at the instance of* " *the Irish*," it must manifestly appear, that this antient example excludes the Doctrine which he meant to support by it, in opposition to Sir Richard Bolton; and therefore, if all these points are duly considered, I think we may very fairly retort his own words (which he exultingly applied to Sir Richard Bolton) upon himself!

himſelf! *viz.* " *Whereupon it muſt needs* " *alſo follow, that the Author's Diſcourſe* " FALLS ALL IN PIECES, *and is nothing* " to the purpoſe that he would have it."

Serjeant Mayart has alſo taken a great deal of needleſs pains to prove " *Ireland* " to be annexed to *the Crown of England,*" and that " the King and Parliament of " England have Power over Ireland," and he cites ſeveral Acts of Parliament, and other Authorities, in pages 64 and 65 of his *Anſwer,* in the *Hibernica,* which clearly prove, indeed, the *former part of the Aſſertion,* (that Ireland is annexed to the Crown of England;) a point which the Iriſh themſelves are ſo far from denying, that they are rather deſirous to maintain it (28). But none of his Authorities afford

(28) Caſe of Ireland, p. 96. " *It has ever been ac-* " *knowledged that the Kingdom of Ireland is inſeparably* " *annexed to the Imperial Crown of England.* The obli- " gation that our Legiſlature lies under by Poining's " Act,

afford the least shadow of Evidence for the latter part of his Assertion, *viz.* the Power of the *English Parliament* over *Ireland.*

P

" Act, 10 Hen. VII. c. 4, makes this *Tye between the* " *two Kingdoms* indissoluble. And we must ever own " it our happiness to be thus annexed to England; " and that the Kings and Queens of England are, by " undoubted Right, *ipso facto*, Kings and Queens of " Ireland. And from hence we may reasonably con- " clude, that, if any Acts of Parliament made in " England should be of force in Ireland, before they " are received there in Parliament, they should be " more especially such Acts as relate to the *Succession* " and *Settlement of the Crown*, and *Recognition* of the " King's Title thereto, and the *Power* and *Juris-* " *diction* of the King. And yet we find, in the *Irish* " Statutes, 28 Hen. VIII. c. 2, *an Act for the Succes-* " *sion of the King and Queen Anne*; and another, chap. 5, " declaring the King to be *supreme Head of the Church* " *of Ireland*; both which Acts had formerly passed in " the Parliament of England. So likewise we find, " amongst the Irish Statutes, *Acts of Recognition of the* " *King's Title to Ireland*, in the reigns of Henry VIII. " Queen Elizabeth, King James, King Charles II. " King William and Queen Mary. By which it ap- " pears, that Ireland, though annexed to the Crown " of England, has always been looked upon to be a " *kingdom complete within itself*, and to have all Juris- " diction to an absolute Kingdom belonging, and " subordinate to no legislative authority on Earth: " Though, it is to be noted, these English Acts, re-

" lating

Ireland. And, becauſe Sir Richard Bolton had allowed that ſuch Laws, made in *England*, as are declaratory of the *Common-Law*, do bind *Ireland* without any confirmation there; (ſee *Hibernica*, p. 27, *&c.*) Serjeant Mayart hopes to avail himſelf of the circumſtance, and obſerves thereupon, "It muſt neceſſarily "follow" (ſays he, p. 76) "that the "Parliament of *England* hath ſtill an in- "fluence upon *Ireland*," *&c.* And a little

"lating to the ſucceſſion, and recognition of the "King's Title, do particularly name Ireland."

See alſo page 33, where the ſame author ſpeaks of "*Ireland's being annexed to*, and, as it were, *united with*, the imperial Crown of England, by ſeveral "Acts of Parliament, both in England and Ireland, "ſince King John's time, But how far this operates, "I ſhall enquire more fully hereafter; I ſhall only, "at preſent, obſerve, that I conceive little more is "effected, by theſe ſtatutes, than that Ireland ſhall "not be *aliened* or *ſeparated* from the King of Eng- "land, who cannot hereby diſpoſe of it otherwiſe than "in *legal ſucceſſion* along with England; and that "whoever is *King of England* is, *ipſo facto*, *King of* "*Ireland*, and the ſubjects of Ireland are obliged to "obey him as their liege Lord."

little farther he adds, " But if it ſhould " happen" (ſays he) " that the Parlia- " ment of *England* ſhould make an ex- " poſition of a Law in force in *Ireland*, " and the Parliament there ſhould make " another, and that it may be different or " contrary to that of *England*, certainly" (ſays he) " *Ireland* muſt be bound (by " the Author's own Rule," meaning Sir Richard Bolton) " by the declaratory " Statute of the Parliament of *Eng-* " *land*."

But Sir Richard Bolton's Rule includes no ſuch Doctrine. For there is nothing unreaſonable in ſuppoſing that the Iriſh ſubjects, without prejudice to their natural Rights and the Privileges of their own Parliament, might receive " *the declara-* " *tory Statute of the Parliament of Eng-* " *land*" as the beſt Expoſition of the Common-Law, which they *before acknow-*

 ledged,

ledged, and *freely accepted* by *their own express assent and desire.* (29)

But

(29) Sir Edward Coke himself bears ample testimony to this. — " Our student must know," (says he,) " that King John, in the 12th year of his reign, " went into Ireland, and there, by the advice of " grave and learned men in the Lawes, whom he carried with him, BY PARLIAMENT, DE COMMUNI " OMNIUM DE HYBERNIA CONSENSU, ordained and " established, that *Ireland* should be governed by *the* " *Laws of England*, which, of many of the *Irish-men*," (for the *common consent* before mentioned must mean that of the *English* settlers) " *according to their own desire*, " *was joyfully accepted and obeyed*, and of many the " same was soon after absolutely refused, preferring " their *Breben* Law before the just and honourable " Lawes of England." 1st Inst. p. 141.

But this subsequent refusal, and preference given to the *Breben Law*, must not be charged to the *native Irish* in general; for Sir John Davis, in his " Dis" coverie of the true causes why Ireland was never en" tirely subdued," &c. demonstrates that the *English Settlers* were *principally* to be blamed for this. He shews, (p. 135,) that " the scopes of land, which " were graunted to the first adventurers, *were too large*, " and the *Liberties* and *Royalties*, which they obtained " therein, *were too great for subjects*." —— And, in p. 144, " that these *Grants* of whole provinces and " petty kingdoms, those few English Lordes pre" tended to be proprietors of all the land, so that " there was no possibility left of *settling the natives in*

" *their*

But let us suppose that, in some such declaratory Act, they had reason to think the

" *their possessions*, and, by consequence, the conquest " became impossible, without the *utter extirpation of* " *all the Irish*; which these English Lordes were not " able to doe, nor perhaps *willing*, if they had been " able." This he afterwards explains, shewing that false notions of private interest, among the *English* Lords, prevented both the conquest, and the introduction of the English Law: They " hoped to become " Lords of those lands which were possessed by the " Irish, whereunto they *pretended title by their large* " *Grants*," &c. (p. 144,) and that therefore " they per-" suaded the King of England (p. 145) that it was " *unfit to communicate the Lawes of England unto them*; " that it was the best policie to holde them as aliens " and enemies, and to prosecute them *with a continual* " *warre*. Hereby they obtained" (says he) " ano-" ther royal Prerogative and power; which was, to " *make Warre and Peace at their pleasure*, in every part " of the kingdom: which gave them an absolute com-" mand over the bodies, lands, and goods," (even) " of the *English* Subjectes heere;" meaning in Ireland, where he wrote. And he adds, in the same page, " And besides" (says he) " the *Irish* inhabit-" ing the lands fully conquered and reduced, being " in *condition of slaves* and villaines, did *render a greater* " *profit and revennew*, than if they had been made *the* " *King's free subjects*. They also feared" (as he declares in the preceding page) " that, if the Irish were " received

the English Exposition improper, and should therefore choose to confirm their own

" received into the King's protection, and made liege-" men and free-subjectes, *the State of England* woulde " *establish them*" (or rather re-establish them) " *in* " *their possessions* by Graunts from the Crown," *&c.* And " The *troth is,*" (says he, in p. 146,) " that " those great English Lords did, to the uttermost of " their power, crosse and withstand the enfranchise-" ment of the Irish, for the causes before expressed."— And he rightly lays " the fault upon the pride, " covetousness, and ill-counsell of the *English* planted " heer, *which in all former ages*" (says he) " have " bin the chief impediments of the final conquest of " Ireland."

On the other hand, he clearly exculpates the *native Irish* from the charge of *wilfully* refusing to be subject to the Laws of England. " But perhaps" (says he, in p. 115) " the *Irishry* in former times did wilfully " refuse to be subiect to the Lawes of England, and " would not be partakers of the benefit thereof, though " the *Crown of England* did desire it; and therefore " they were reputed Aliens, Out-lawes, and Enemies. " ASSUREDLY THE CONTRARIE DOTH APPEARE, as " wel by the Charters of Denization, purchased by " the Irish IN ALL AGES, as by a petition preferred " by them to the King, anno 2 Ed. III. desiring that " an Act *might passe in Ireland,* whereby ALL THE " IRISHRIE might be inabled to use and injoy the " *Lawes of England,* without purchasing of *particular* " *Denizations.*"

And,

own sense of it by the Authority of their *own Parliament*, surely the latter would be

And, in p. 117, he adds: — "I am well assured, "that *the Irishrie* DID DESIRE *to be* admitted to the "benefit of the Law, not only in this petition exhibi- "ted to King Edw. III. but *by all their submissions* "made to King Richard II. and to the Lord Thomas "of Lancaster, before the warres of the two Houses; "and afterwards to the Lord Leonard Gray and Sir An- "thony St. Leger, when K. Henry VIII. began to "reform this kingdom. In particular, the Birnes of "of the Mountaines, in the 34th of Hen. VIII. de- "sire that their countrey might be made Shire-ground; "and called the County of Wicklow: And, in the "23d of Hen. VIII. O. Donnel doth covenant with "Sir William Skeffington, *Quod si Dominus Rex velit* "*reformare Hiberniam,*" (whereof, it should seem, he made some doubt,) "that *hee and his people would* "GLADLY *bee governed by the Lawes of England.*"

These quotations sufficiently demonstrate the *willingness* of the native *Irish* to adopt the *English* Laws and Constitution, and that the denial of such a reasonable desire was the just cause of their almost continual rebellions and bloody wars against the *English* Settlers. However, in the reign of King James I. *the Irishry* were restored to their just Rights, "and the benefit "and protection of the Law of England communica- "ted TO ALL, AS WELL IRISH AS ENGLISH, WITH- "OUT DISTINCTION OR RESPECT OF PERSONS," &c. (p. 264.) And Sir John Davies himself was one of the judges employed in that most grateful business to

be binding in Ireland, and *not the English Statute*, as Serjeant Mayart supposes; for

to a benevolent man; I mean the "*Visitations of Justice, whereby the just and* HONOURABLE LAW OF "ENGLAND was imparted and communicated to *all* "*the Irishry.*" (P. 265.) And he informs us, in the same page, that "*the common people* were taught, by "the Justices of Assise, that *they were* FREE SUB-"JECTS *to the Kings of England*, and not Slaves and "Vassals to their pretended Lords: That the *Cut*-"*tings, Cosheries, Sessings*, and other extortions of "their Lords, were UNLAWFUL, and that they should "not any more submit themselves thereunto, since "they were now under the protection of so just and "mighty a Prince, as both would and could protect "them from al' wrongs and oppressions. They gave" (says he) "A WILLING EAR unto these lessons; and "thereupon the greatnesse and power of those Irish "Lords over the people sodainly fell and vanished, "when their oppressions and extortions were taken "away, which did maintain their greatness," &c. In p. 262, he informs us, that Sir Edmund Pelham and himself were "*the first Justices of Assise that ever* "*sat in those countries*;" (speaking particularly of Tyrone and Tirconnell;) "and in that circuit" (says he) "we visited all the shires of that province: be-"sides which, visitation, though it were somewhat "distastfull to the Irish Lords, *was sweet and most* "*welcome to the common people*; who, albeit they were "rude and barbarous, yet did they *quickly apprehend* "*the difference* betweene the tiranny and oppression under

for there is no example of an *Irish* Act of Parliament being set aside by the Autho-

Q rity

" under which they lived before, and *the just govern-* " *ment* and protection which we promised unto them " for the time to come."

Thus the common people of *the Irishry* were at length restored to that equality, in the eye of the law, to which they were justly entitled (though shamefully deprived of it) from the earliest time that the English began to be known in that kingdom, even from the first establishment of the English Conquerors; for Sir John Davies shews, from Matthew Paris's History, that " King Henry II. *before his return out of Ire-* " *land*, held a Counsell, or Parliament, at *Lissemore*, " where the Laws of England were, *by all*, *willingly* " *received*; ubi leges Angliæ AB OMNIBUS *sunt gra-* " *tanter receptæ*, et juratoria cautione præstita confir- " matæ:" p. 100. And he informs us, in the next page, that " King Henrie the Third did graunt and " transmit the *like Charter of Liberties to his subjects of* " *Ireland*, as himself and his Father had graunted to " *the Subjects of England*, as appeareth" (says he) " by another Record in the Tower, 1 Hen. III. " Pat. m. 13." And he cites also a writ of the 12th year of the same King, commanding the Lord Justice of Ireland to cause *the Charter of King John* to be read and confirmed by Parliament; and again, that " the " same King, by Letters Patent under the Great-Seal " of England, *did confirme the establishment* of the *Eng-* " *lish Laws* made by King John," and that all Writs of *the Common Law* should have course there as in Eng-

land

rity of the *English* Parliament, which Serjeant Mayart allows: "Neither is it "to be imagined" (says he in p. 199) "that the Kings and Parliaments in Eng-"land will ever *avoid any Laws made in* "*Ireland* without a good and just cause, "*since they have not done any such things* "*for about four hundred years*, which is "time enough to have experience of "their honour and justice," &c.

And he afterwards uses this plea concerning the Honour and Justice of the English Parliament, as an inducement for the Irish to be bound by it; "and seeing" (says he in p. 191) "that, for above "400 years, they have never done hurt "to Ireland, &c. therefore we may *well* "*trust*

land — "*Quod* OMNIA BREVIA *de* COMMUNI JURE, "*quæ currunt in Anglia, similiter currant in Hibernia,*" &c. Thus it appears, that all *Irish* Subjects, without distinction, are entitled, according to the clearest and most unquestionable testimony, to all the Rights, Immunities, and Advantages, of *Magna Charta* and the *English* Common Law.

" *trust them* hereafter," *&c.* And again, in p. 192, " But we all know" (says he) " with *what great consultation, delibera-* " *tion, and knowledge of things, and the* " *circumstances of them, the Kings and* " *Parliaments of England* have still or- " dered their affairs, *&c.* And we may," (says he,) " as all our ancestors have " done, *trust to their wisdom, justice, and* " *judgement*, as a *sufficient hedge* and secu- " rity for us." But, surely, no People, who have the use of reason or common-sense, would be induced by *such an argument* to submit themselves implicitly to a Parliament, in which they have no Share of Power or *Representation*; though, indeed, it may be alleged, in behalf of this writer and his argument, that Parliaments, before his time, were, *in general*, less corrupt than they have been since, if we except the Parliaments of Richard II. and Queen Mary; but, in these latter times, " *we all know with* " *what*

"*what great consultation, deliberation, and*
"*knowledge of things, &c. &c. &c.*"

If it had been possible for the *Irish* Subjects to have given up to Serjeant Mayart this contested point, concerning the necessity of *a due Representation in the Legislature,* without giving up, at the same time, *all due Limitation of Government,* and consequently *all pretensions to their natural Freedom,* this advice of his might have been esteemed excusable!

But it is *Representation alone* which forms the Basis, the superiority, and the essential difference, of the *English* Constitution of State, from all others! For, in countries where *this is wanting,* or where it is become *totally corrupted,* it makes but little difference, to the bulk of the people, whether the executive part of government be in the hands of one, of a few, or of many; *viz.* of an Emperor,

Emperor, of a Triumvirate, or of a Senate of Nobles or proud Patricians, (as among the Romans, at different periods of time). The adminiſtration of each of theſe orders of power, reſpectively, is almoſt equally arbitrary, uncertain, and dangerous to the community; to which the Hiſtories of all monarchical as well as ariſtocratical Governments (I mean thoſe that are merely or too nearly ſuch) bear ſufficient teſtimony: ſo that *the Repreſentation of the people* is the grand point of diſtinction, the fundamental principle, whereby the equity and ſafety of the *Engliſh* Government is to be meaſured, when we compare it with ſuch Governments as either that of France, or that of Poland.

I have already given ſome ſpecimens of *French* Government and *French* Law in my Preface, it being neceſſary that *Britiſh* Subjects ſhould be well aware of the

the Nature and Tendency of that Law which has so lately received the solemn Sanction even of our own Legislature,(30) as

(30) The late Act for establishing the Laws of *France* in the most extensive Province of the *British* Empire must indeed seem very strange and unnatural to the genius of *Englishmen* in general; especially when we consider that even the *French* Inhabitants of that Province themselves are zealous for the "*Privileges of English Subjects*;" which plainly appears by some Expressions in their late Address to the Governor on that occasion: and we may, therefore, rest assured that they are not, in general, so ignorant, and void of common-sense, as really to prefer the Laws of *France* to the *equitable* Constitution of *England*, howsoever they may have been misrepresented. We must, nevertheless, except a few French Seigneurs, who, having already been allowed *greater exclusive Privileges* than are consistent with the safety and freedom of their poor neighbours and fellow-subjects, would rather wish to promote the *French* Laws and Customs (which permit such an unjust Vassalage) than the equitable Laws of *England*: and we may likewise except the Priests, and some other absolute Bigots to the Romish Religion, who, being entangled in *the Slavery of antichristian Principles* and "*the Doctrines of Devils*," are ready to submit to any *temporal* conditions whatsoever for the sake of that *spiritual*, or rather *Satanical*, Bribe, which was wickedly thrown out to them on this occasion: I mean the setting up their *adulterated* Religion as the *established Church of that Province* (with a legal

as being proper to be renewed and enforced in a certain Province of the British Empire! And the Hon. Mr. Justice Barrington, in his Observations on the ancient Statutes, has also, in just abhorrence of the French Law, cited several "Fundamental Maxims" (31) of it, "upon which the King's Prerogative is founded, which" (as he justly remarks) "may not only be matter of some curiosity to an Englishman, "but,

legal Right to collect Tythes, *&c.*) *by national authority*. This was the more unjust and inexcusable, because the Romanists had no reason to complain of that Toleration which they so freely enjoyed before. In a note on p. 125, where I have occasion to mention the defects of some *supposed* Statutes, I have added some examples (which naturally occurred thereupon) concerning the abominable Tyranny and Wickedness of the *adulterous* Church of *Rome*; and these, I trust, will sufficiently justify the severity of my expressions against that *antichristian* Church. See also my "Remarks on "several very important Prophecies," part 2, p. 18, and part 4, p. 34.

(31) "Si veut le Roy, si veut le Loi." The King's Will is Law! Some of the pernicious effects of this detestable maxim I have already shewn in my Preface.

" but, by comparison, may make him " thankful for *the noble Constitution to* " *which he is happily born*. A Cappa- " docian" (says he) " may indeed re- " fuse, from custom and long usage, to " exchange a despotic for a more free " Government; but I can never be per- " suaded" (says this benevolent Gentleman) " but that there is *a necessary con-* " *nexion between Slavery and Misery*, and " *between Freedom and Happiness*. Se- " neca" (says he) " nobly inforces the " communication of *Liberty to the Sub-* " *ject*, from *the Safety* it procures *to the* " *King*: (32) Errat si quis existimat tu- " tum esse ibi Regem, ubi nihil a Rege " tutum est; securitas securitate mutuâ " paciscenda est." p. 179. Now, this necessary

(32) This was the uniform Doctrine of all the antient constitutional Lawyers of England, and especially of the great Chancellor Fortescue, whose opinion I have expressly quoted, and added some farther observations upon the same point, in a Note on page 7 of this *Declaration*, Part I.

neceſſary *mutual ſecurity* can only be inſured by *a free Repreſentation of the People* in the Legiſlature; and therefore the learned Author of this excellent remark will readily allow, (I truſt,) when he comes to conſider theſe arguments, that he himſelf was not ſufficiently upon his guard, in another part of his uſeful work, (p. 141,) where he had occaſion to mention the *Iriſh Laws*; having there unfortunately adopted the miſtaken doctrine of Lord Coke, about binding the *Subjects of Ireland* by *Engliſh* Statutes, " *if Ireland is mentioned.*" But it is certainly very natural for a gentleman regularly bred to the profeſſion of the Law to be leſs circumſpect when he follows ſo great an authority as Sir Edward Coke, who is *generally*, and for the moſt part *juſtly*, eſteemed the Oracle of the Engliſh Law.

Mr. Barrington is commenting on the Ordinance of 17 Edw. I. *pro ſtatu Hiberniæ*; and, after informing us that it is not found in the Collection of Iriſh Statutes, which begin only with *the Ordinance of Kilkenny*, in the 3d of Edw. II. he adds, " There can be no doubt," (ſays he,) " however, that this Law " extends to Ireland, *if not repealed by* " *ſome Iriſh Act of Parliament*; (33) " as

(33) This Sentence contains an implied acknowledgement that a Law made in *England*, relating to the Government of *Ireland*, may be " *repealed by an Iriſh* " *Act of Parliament*;" and if this be allowed, (which it certainly ought to be,) there can be no room to ſuppoſe the *Iriſh* Subjects bound by an *Engliſh* Act " *if* " *Ireland is mentioned*;" for, wherein is the force or *binding* of the *Engliſh* Act if the *Iriſh* are allowed a Right to repeal it? Such *binding* amounts to nothing: we may as well ſay that an *Engliſh* Act *binds* the Emperor of *Morocco* and his Subjects, or the wild *Arabs*, " *when eſpecially named*," ſince it can *bind* no longer than while they ſhall be willing to ſubmit to it! But, that the *Iriſh* Subjects really have a *Right* to *repeal* an *Engliſh Act* relating to their own internal Government, (if we may with propriety apply the word *repeal* to Acts

"as by *Poining's Law*, in the time of "Henry the Seventh, all PRECEDENT "(34) ENGLISH STATUTES are made "to bind in *Ireland*." And he remarks thereupon, in a note, that "*subsequent* "Statutes only bind *if Ireland is men-* "*tioned*; as for *Wales*," (continues he,) "all Statutes are now made to extend "to it, whether *mentioned or not*, by a "clause inserted in the middle of 20 "Geo. II. cap. xlii." &c. But the true reason why this doctrine may be applied to *Wales* with propriety and *justice*, (and yet not to *Ireland* without *injustice*,) is, because the *Welchmen* give their *assent* to the *English* Laws by their Representatives in the *English* Parliament, whereas the *assent* of the *Irish*, *which is equally*

Acts that were originally defective and void for want of the *Irish* assent,) is clearly proved by Mr. Mollyneux, in his *Case of Ireland*, page 76.

(34) Here the Hon. Mr. Barrington confirms what is before laid down in pages 91 and 92, concerning the effect of Poining's Law.

essential, cannot be known, in a *legal* manner, but by the voice of *their own* parliamentary *Representatives*; so that the very reason why all *English* Statutes "*extend to Wales, whether named or not*" forbids the application of the like Doctrine to *Ireland*: and, as the opinion of the Judges, in the 19th of Hen. VI. and in the 2d of Rich. III. before cited, in favour of Ireland, was founded on *this very reason*, ("quia non hic habent milites parliamenti,") I hope the same will be thought sufficient to justify my dissent, as well from Mr. Barrington as from the great Author whom he seems to have followed in this matter, I mean Lord Coke himself, whose assertion I propose to examine still more closely, before I conclude this 2d part of my Declaration.

The Hon. Mr. Justice Barrington also observes, in p. 145, that "there have "been

"been great and learned controversies "between Molyneux and others, with "regard to an English Act of Parliament binding in *Ireland*; and Molyneux," (says he,) "who contends it "should not, hath *argued strongly* from "an *English* Statute's not being supposed "to extend to *Ireland* before Poyning's "Act in the reign of Henry the Seventh," *&c.* — and a very *strong argument* it is! which, I hope, hath already been shewn. But the Hon. Mr. Barrington proceeds to cite, from the Parliament-Rolls of the 21st of Edw. I. a memorandum of a very unwarrantable exertion of Royal-Prerogative, by that monarch, *viz.* his sending a copy of *the Ordinance* (35) (for I cannot properly call it a Statute)

(35) The Hon. Mr. Barrington, in p. 41, very justly remarks, concerning the Statute of Merton, in the 20th year of Hen. III. that the said "Statute, as well "as many others of this century, seems to be only "an Ordinance; the difference" (says he) "between "an

a Statute) *de malefactoribus in Parcis* into Ireland, with an order to the Chief-Justice

"an Ordinance and Statute (according to Sir Edward "Coke) consisting in this, that the Ordinance wants "the consent of *one component part* of the Legislature, "which, is, in all instances, *that of the Commons*." Now, this seems to be exactly the case of the Act in question, of the 21st of Edw. I. *de malefactoribus in Parcis*; for, though the Act itself declares that it was ordained by the King "at his Parliament,"* and "*at the instance of the Nobles of his realm*," yet the assent of the *Commons* is not *expressed*; which was very well known, even at that time, to be necessary, as the assent expressed in the Acts of the preceding year sufficiently demonstrates; *viz.* "Our Lord the King, "*in his full Parliament, and by his common Council*, hath "ordained," &c. Statute *de defensione juris*, 20 E, 1. Again, in the Statute of Vouchers, "By his *common* "*Council* hath ordained," &c. Again, in the Statute of Waste, "Our Lord the King, in his *full* Parlia-"ment, holden, &c. by a *general Council* hath or-"dained:" so that a proper Form of declaring the *Assent* of the Commons, even at that time, was very well established, notwithstanding that many Statutes are deficient therein, and consequently are exceptionable in point of authority; as for instance, the Statute *de Escheatoribus*, of the 29th year of this reign, seems to be thus defective; for though it is dated very speciously,

* "Our Lord the King, *at his Parliament* after Easter, the 21st "year of his reign, at the instance of the Nobles of his realm, hath "granted and commanded to be from henceforth firmly observed," &c.

Juſtice of *Ireland*, to enforce it: and he remarks thereupon: — " This note fully " proves"

ſpeciouſly, (like the Act in queſtion, *de malefactoribus in parcis,)* " *at the Parliament* of our Lord the King " at Lincoln," *&c.* yet it ſeems only to have been " *agreed to* by the Privy-Council, or the King's Coun-" cil ; — " by *his Council* it was *agreed*, and alſo " commanded by the King himſelf" (" *per Conſilium* " *Regis* concordatum eſt coram Domino Rege, ipſo " Rege conſentiente et illud extunc fieri et obſervari " precipiente," *&c.)* — ſo that it was apparently e-nacted and ordained only *by the King and his Council*, without the leaſt mention of the *Conſent* of the Parlia-ment, or of the *common Council* of the Kingdom, and ſeems therefore to have been a mere *Order in Council*, though artfully dated, " *at the Parliament*," in order to give it the appearance of Law. Sir Edward Coke, in his 4th inſt. p. 51, gives ſeveral inſtances of ſup-poſed Statutes that had been repealed or diſaffirmed, (wanting the Aſſent of the Commons,) which were ne-vertheleſs publiſhed and enforced as real Statutes ; *viz.* 5 R. II. c. 5. ſtat. 2, touching enquiries of Hereſies, and 2 H. IV. c. 15, againſt pretended Hereticks, giving pow-er to the Biſhop, or Ordinary, " to convent before " him or *impriſon* any perſon ſuſpected of Hereſie ;" and ordaining (contrary to the Laws of God) that " an obſtinate Heretick" (or any perſon whom an ig-norant popiſh Enthuſiaſt was pleaſed to call ſo) " ſhall " be *burned before the people* ;" both which, as Sir Edward Coke remarks, were *diſavowed* by the Com-mons, and (yet) the pretended Acts *printed* (4 inſt. p.

51,

"proves" (says he) "that it was supposed "the King, by his sole authority, could "then

51, and 3 inst. p. 40 and 41). Also 2 Hen. V. *cap.* 7, (which Sir Edward Coke, by mistake, calls *cap.* 6,) "against Preachers (was) disavowed the next Par- "liament by the Commons, for that *they never as- "sented*, and yet the *supposed* Act (was) *printed.*" (4 Inst. p. 51.) By such notorious *treachery* and *dishonesty* did the Zealots of the Romish Church introduce the papal Tyranny into *England.*

Sir Edward Coke, in his 3d Inst. (pages 40 and 41,) clearly proves, from the Parliament-Rolls and other Records, the *fraudulent* introduction of the above-mentioned Act, in the 5th of Rich. II. by a popish Prelate*, who at that time was Lord-Chancellor: And

* Sir Edward Coke calls him "*John Braibrook,*" 3 Inst. p. 41; but, according to Bishop Godwin, his name was "*Robert Bray- "brook;*" (*De Præsulibus Angliæ Com.* p. 186.) but both of them testify that he was Bishop of London, as well as Lord Chancellor. Among the *blessed* effects of his *pious* fraud the following are reported by Sir Edward Coke, 3d Inst. p. 40. —— "By colour of this *sup- "posed* Act," (5 Rich. II.) certain persons that held *that Images "were not to be worshipped,* &c. were holden in *strong prison,* until "they (to redeem their vexation) miserably yielded before these "Masters of Divinity to take an Oath, and did *swear to worship "Images*; which was against the moral and eternal Law of Almighty "God!" This and many other such instances of hardened Apostacy in popish Professors sufficiently justify our applying to the *papal Tyranny,* in general, that Prophecy of the Apostle Paul concerning the "*Man of Sin,*" that was to be *revealed,* "the Son of Perdition, "who opposeth and exalteth himself above all that is called God, or "that is worshipped; so that he, as God, sitteth in the temple of "God, shewing himself that he is God" (2 Thess. ii. 3 to 6); and "whom

" then introduce any *English* Law ; and " will that authority" (says he) " be

S " lessened

And the same learned author thereupon directs us to " *mark well the manner of the penning the Act:* for, see- " ing" (says he) " the Commons did not assent there- " unto, the words of the Act be, *It is ordained and* " *assented in this present Parliament, that,* &c. And so " it was, being but by the King and the Lords."

The same rule enables us to judge concerning the authenticity of many other ancient Acts, wherein the *Assent of the Commons* is not particularly mentioned, and yet they are published. The constitutions called *Statutum de Bigamis*, for instance, are declared *to have been* " *set forth in the Parliament* after Michaelmas," *&c.* " Editæ fuerunt apud Westm. in parliamento post " festum sancti Michaelis," *&c.* (Mag. Char. cum statutis quæ antiqua vocantur, *&c.* p. 104, b. Ed. 1556.) But when we " *mark well the manner of the pen-* " *ning the Act,*" according to Sir Edward Coke's rule, it appears to be very deficient in parliamentary Authority, though he himself has taken great pains to prove its authenticity. He remarks, that " these words in " the 1st chapter (concordatum est per justiciarios et " alios

" whom the Lord shall consume with the Spirit of his mouth, and " shall *destroy* with the brightness of *his Coming* ;" (verse 8.) — O! that all those persons, whose hearts are not yet entirely " *seared with* " *the hot iron*" of popish Enthusiasm, may duly consider these glaring instances of popish craft in opposition to the Laws of God, and consequently the apparent danger of adhering to that church which has so notoriously perverted the Doctrines of the Gospel ; lest they should be found in communion with the Enemies of Christ at his glorious *Coming!*

" leſſened by the concurrence of the " two Houſes of Parliament?" But this

" alios ſapientes *de Concilio Regni)* prove it to be by " Authority of Parliament; for *Concilium Regni,*" (ſays he) " *is the Lords and Commons,* LEGALLY CALLED " COMMUNE CONCILIUM REGNI." 2d Inſt. p. 267. But, even according to this argument, the word " COMMUNE" is apparently wanting, to make up what he himſelf allows to be the LEGAL expreſſion for THE LORDS AND COMMONS; and, if we duly conſider the words which immediately follow, it muſt appear, that the " *ſapientes de Concilio Regni,*" &c. here mentioned, were only ſuch particular *ſapientes* as held *judicial places,* (" qui conſuetudines et *uſum judiciorum* hactenus habu- " erunt"); ſo that the expreſſion cannot, with propriety, be ſuppoſed to include the *whole repreſentative Body of the Commons,* as well as the Lords, *&c.* but merely *the Judges,* and ſuch Lords, Prelates, and others, as held *judicial places,* and were of the *King's Council,* mentioned in the preamble, *viz.* In præſentia, *&c.* quorundam epiſcoporum Angliæ, et *aliorum, de Concilio Regis,* which Sir Edward Coke (by what authority I cannot gueſs) is pleaſed to call a " *Committee* " *of both Houſes,*" though it can mean nothing more than a meeting of the *King's Privy-Council*; and the ſame may be ſaid of that ſecond meeting, afterwards mentioned, " *coram Domino Rege et Concilio ſuo,*" wherein the ſaid Conſtitutions were again read *(auditæ et publicatæ)* and *ordered to be ingroſſed and obſerved*; " quod " in ſcripturam redigerentur ad perpetuam memoriam, " et *quod firmiter obſerventur*:" which (be pleaſed to remark) is the principal *enacting* or *enforcing clauſe* of this

this by no means invalidates *the juſtice* of Mr. Molyneux's argument, while *the*

S 2 *injuſtice,*

this Act: And, therefore, when we conſider that the ſame was *agreed to*, or *ordained*, by THE JUDGES *as well as others*, (" tam *Juſticiarii* quam alii concordaverunt " quod in ſcripturam," *&c.*) we may be aſſured that the meeting was *not the Parliament*, (in which the *Judges*, as ſuch, have not any vote or voice at all, except that of *adviſing*,) but merely the *King's Privy-Council:* and therefore Judge *Shard*, as cited by Lord Coke, had, ſurely, reaſon on his ſide, when he, " *beholding the manner of the penning of this Act*," (compare this with Lord Coke's own Rule, to the ſame purpoſe, abovementioned,) " *was of opinion that it* " *was no Act of Parliament*," though Sir Edward Coke was pleaſed to cenſure him, ſaying, that " the contrary " is holden by many expreſs Authorities, both before " and after him." (2d Inſt. p. 267.) But what Authorities can be equal to the *internal evidence* of the Act itſelf, according to his own rule, " *Mark well the man-* " *ner of the penning?* &c. For, though it may have been allowed the force of an Act, in judicial proceedings, as well as in the writings of ſome reſpectable commentators, yet this is nothing but the natural conſequence of its having been publiſhed and printed, without remarks, among the other Acts, * agreeable to the intention of thoſe who unlawfully promoted it. But Lord Shard declared from the Bench, in the Aſſiſes at Wincheſter,

* The *undue Authority*, acquired by ſuch impoſitions, was ſtill more notorious, in the credit that has been given, even by the Legiſlature itſelf, to the three other *falſe* Statutes before-mentioned againſt (what the Papiſts call) Hereſy: Two of them are expreſsly recited, and formally

injustice, of which he complains, is ſtill continued; *viz.* the inequitable pretenſion to *bind* the Subjects of *Ireland* by Laws made *without their Aſſent*, and this

Wincheſter, (anno 30th E. 3.) that *this never was a Statute*. Lib. Aſſiſarum, p. 173." "*Shard.* Negativa nihil "implicat. Et ceo que vous parles del' Statut *de Bi-* "*gamis*, ceo ne fuit unquam aſcun *Statut*."

Another objection againſt this *ſuppoſed* Statute is the apparent evil intention of the 5th Article, "*de Bi-* "*gamis*," (from whence it has acquired its title,) which was, to acknowledge a *foreign* popiſh Law, as if it were already (without interpoſition of Parliament) of legal *force* in *England*, and needed only ſome ſmall explanation, with reſpect to the manner of putting it in execution; an idea this, which all *free* Engliſh Parliaments, even in *popiſh times*, moſt zealouſly oppoſed! But, above all, the *Iniquity* of the *foreign Decree itſelf*, which is introduced by this 5th Article, affords the moſt ample argument againſt the *whole Statute*, as it ſeems to have been drawn up principally for purpoſe of enforcing, and ſmuggling in, amongſt other

mally repealed by an Act of Parliament in the the 1ſt of Edward VI. (cap. 12. §. 3.) as if they had *really* been *Statutes* ordained by the Authority of the whole Legiſlature; and all the three falſe Statutes together are recited, acknowledged, and revived, by another Act of Parliament, in the 1. & 2. P. & M. (cap. 6.) and are yet again expreſsly intitled *Statutes*, and as ſuch are formally repealed by a third Act of Parliament in the 1ſt of Eliz. c. 1. §. 15. But yet theſe ſeveral great Authorities by no means invalidate the Evidence which Sir Edward Coke has produced, to prove that the ſaid three wicked Ordinances were *really no Statutes*.

this even without any exception or just distinction concerning *external* or *internal* Government; for the *Irish* themselves

do

ther articles, that *diabolical* popish Decretal of Pope Gregory IX. for discouraging lawful *Marriages* of Widows or Widowers! The Marriages of *the Clergy* had been absolutely forbid || about 200 years before, and those who were already married *forcibly separated* from their wives, * (in open contradiction to the Laws of God,) by a Decree of Pope Gregory VII. which was still further enforced by his successors; and the

Clergy

|| As the "*forbidding to marry*" is ranked by the apostle Paul amongst the "*Doctrines of Devils*," (1 Tim. iv. 1.) so the papal Antichrist, in very early times, began to discourage the *Marriages* of the Clergy: but Pope Gregory VII. alias *Hildebrand*, a Monster in Iniquity, (to prove which Dr. Cave has cited unexceptionable authorities, *Hist. Liter.* p. 535.) more openly *revealed* "*the man* "*of sin*" in the 11th Century, and, amongst other notorious manifestations of most impious Tyranny, "made a Decree" (in 1074) that, "from that time forward, it shou'd no more be lawfull for "Priestes *to marrye*," &c. *Becon's Reliques of Rome*, p. 32 *b*. This was apparently a *contrary Doctrine* to what St. Paul preached, and consequently it subjects the Roman See to the *Anathema* of that Apostle! "Though we, or an Angel from Heaven, preach any other Gospel "unto you than that which we have preached unto you, let him be "accursed." Gal. i. 8 & 9. The Marriage of the Clergy had never before been forbidden except among the worst of Heretics, but had been allowed by the whole Church of Christ, from the time of the Apostles, for above 1000 years, down to this unhappy Century: and, with respect to *Ireland* in particular, Sir Edward Coke informs us, that, "at a Synod holden *in Ireland*, by *St. Patrick*, their Apostle, it "was unanimously agreed that *Irish Priests* should have Wives." 4 Inst. p. 356.

* Becon's Reliques of Rome, p. 32 *b*.

do not deny the propriety of the pretension in the former case. The exertion

Clergy were compelled at length to submit to that unnatural Tyranny, by a variety of the most unjust and cruel laws and oppressions † that satanical malice could possibly devise, in the several ecclesiastical Synods of that and the following century.

But the Decree against *Bigamy* was aimed at the *Laity* as well as Clergy ; since every Layman that could *read* was (before) entitled to the *Benefit of Clergy*, when convicted of some particular offences ; which privilege was by this Decree taken away from all persons called *bigami*, or who had been twice married successively, ‡ the principal purpose of this new popish Ordinance being to cast an odium and restraint upon *lawful* second marriages, and confound them with the *real* Felony of having two wives at one time. Thus

† See, for instance, the several Decrees of a Council, held at London by Anselm, Archbishop of Canterbury, in 1108, upon this subject, to oblige the Clergy to forsake their *lawful* wives, who were mentioned by the Council as *Concubines*, and were ordered to be delivered up to the Bishops as *Adulteresses*, together with all the goods of those unfortunate husbands, who persisted in their natural affection! Tenth and last Article: " Omnia vero mobilia lapsorum posthac " Presbyterorum, Diaconorum," *&c.* (meaning the goods of those who *continued to visit their wives,)* " tradentur Episcopis, et *Concu-* " *bina,* cum rebus suis, velut *Adultera*." Howel's *Synopsis Canonum, &c.* vol. 1. p. 88.

‡ Bigamie (says Sir William Staunford, in his " Plees del Coron." p. 134) " est un *counterplee* a Clergie," (Lambard calls it an " *un-* " *godly* and *popish Counterplea*," Eiren. p. 555,) " s. a dire, que " cestui, qui demaunde le privilege de son Clergy, fuist espouse a un " feme, a tiel lieu, deynz tiel dioces, et que *le dit feme morust*, et ad " *espouse auter feme*," &c.

tion of royal Prerogative, above-mentioned, was certainly *illegal*, and therefore muſt be eſteemed *a bad precedent*; for Mr. Barrington himſelf, who cites it, does not pretend to juſtify it; and I know that he will as readily allow, that one *bad precedent* cannot juſtify another; ſo that his *adding* ſtill more precedents of the ſame kind *adds no weight* to his argument, becauſe the *authority* of *Precedents* muſt always be weighed and governed by *Firſt-Principles* and *conſtitutional Law*; otherwiſe we ſhould be liable to adopt the moſt dangerous doctrines, ſince there is nothing *ſo bad* but that a *Precedent* may be found for it!

The

Thus the intention of the Romiſh Church was apparently *diabolical*; under a falſe pretence of extraordinary purity, to diſcourage *lawful Marriages*, and thereby enſnare mankind, through their natural frailties, into *real pollutions*: and it is notorious that the popiſh tenet of "*forbidding to marry*" is one of the diſtinguiſhing *ſcriptural marks of* ANTICHRIST!

The ſecond precedent of this nature, which he has produced for the ſame purpoſe, ſtill helps to confirm my obſervation on the other ſide of the queſtion: for this precedent is nothing leſs than the Order of "King Charles the Firſt, in "the 3d year of his reign, to the Trea-"ſurers and Chancellors of the Exche-"quer, both of England and Ireland, "by which they are directed to increaſe "the duties upon Iriſh exports; which "*ſhews*" (ſays he) "that *it was then* "*imagined*, the King could tax Ireland "by his Prerogative, without the inter-"vention of Parliament." — Now, the precedent "*ſhews*" indeed (as Mr. Barrington juſtly remarks) "*that it was* "*then imagined*," &c. that is, it *ſhews* that this falſe doctrine "*was then ima-*"*gined*" by the King and thoſe wretched Courtiers, who, either through ignorance, or wickedneſs, or both, betrayed him with

with their *unlawful* counsels; but it by no means "shews" that such an arbitrary proceeding was really *Law* at that time, any more than it is at present! for the very same volume of Rymer's Fœdera, (*viz.* tome xviii.) that contains the above-mentioned precedent, contains also other precedents of the like authority, "*which* equally *shew that it was* "*then imagined the King could tax*" EVEN ENGLAND ITSELF "*by his Prerogative,* "*without the intervention of Parliament.*" — See "A Declaration of his Majes-"ty's cleere *intention* in requiring the "ayde of his loving subjects in *that way* "*of Loane* (36) *which is now intended* "*by his Highness.*" Tome xviii. p. 764.

T Nay,

(36) The compulsive means, used on this occasion, to extort money from the people, sufficiently demonstrate that "*the way of Loane, which*" (was then) "*intended by his Highness,*" amounted to an *exaction* of the most notorious nature! Many people were imprisoned, and many others pressed into the land and sea service, for refusing to contribute. See Rushworth's Collection,

Nay, "*it was then imagined,*" (it seems,) by those *disloyal* persons who falsely called

Collection, vol. 1, p. 426. Sir Thomas Wentworth (afterwards Lord Strafford) was one of the sufferers on this occasion, for "*he was imprisoned*, by the Lords of "the Council, *for refusing the royal Loan.*" Supplement to the new and general Biographical Dictionary, p. 474. "His Majesty *demanded* of the City of London the loan of an hundred thousand pounds." Rushworth's Collection, vol. 1, p. 419. If such precedents were to be admitted, or allowed any weight at all, in this argument, the very same reign would afford *precedents* sufficient to render the King of England as despotic as the Emperor of Morocco! In the fourth year of this reign, "the King's Commission" was issued "to "the Lord-Treasurer and Barons of the Exchequer, "and to the Customers of the Ports," to collect Tonnage and Poundage without authority of Parliament. — "Know ye, that we, by advice of *our Lords,*" (that is, the *Lords of his Council,* mentioned in the beginning of the Commission,) "declare *our Will,* that all those "duties be levied and collected as they were in the "time of our father, and in such manner *as we shall* "*appoint:* and, if any person refuse to pay, *then our* "*Will is,* that the Lord-Treasurer *shall commit to pri-* "*son* such, so refusing, till they conform themselves: "and *we give full Power* to all our officers, from time "to time, to give assistance to the farmers of the same, "AS FULLY AS WHEN THEY WERE COLLECTED BY "AUTHORITY OF PARLIAMENT." Rushworth, vol. 1, p. 669. Here the Neglect of the "*Authority of Par-* "*liament*"

led themselves "*the King's Friends*," that the King could not only *tax* his English Subjects by his Prerogative, but that he could also *seize*, *imprison*, *try*, *and even* HANG *them*, *by martial Law*, *without Judge or Jury!*

The very same volume of Rymer's Fœdera (tome xviii.) affords several authentic *precedents* for delegating such unlimited Power by the King's Commission! *viz.* one for the county of Sussex, p. 751; another for the whole county of Kent, p. 763; and a third for the town and county of Southampton, p. 804: (37) and

"*liament*" is openly avowed, though the forgetful Monarch was bound under a solemn oath, at his coronation, to maintain the Laws of the land!

(37) The Commissioners were impowered not only to use *martial Law* "against soldiers or mariners," but also against "OTHER *dissolute persons*, *joining with them*, "or *any of them*;" whereby, under *the latter denomination*, a way was opened to render all other persons (besides soldiers and mariners) liable to the uncertain decisions

and therefore, as it would be *partial* to admit an *arbitrary precedent* as an evidence on one side of the question, *(i..e.* against *Ireland,)* without weighing, at the same time, the *similar precedents* in the same unfortunate reign, which equally affect the other side of the question, (I mean the Privileges of the English

decisions and hasty rigour of martial Law! Any man whatever might be *unjustly* charged as a *dissolute person*, &c. and the *accusation alone*, whether *true* or *false*, was sufficient to divest the person accused of all the privileges of an English subject, at the very time when he stood most in need of them! So that, if the King's Commissioners should happen to dislike any particular person, within the county, or limits of the jurisdiction, expressed in their Commission, it was possible for them to promote *such an accusation*, and thereby render themselves *Judges in their own cause*; since the King's Commission (contrary to his Majesty's most solemn engagement, before God, at his coronation) deprived the *accused* subject of a legal Trial and the due Process of the Law, the only defence of *the innocent*, by substituting an *illegal Process* in lieu of it! And the horror of this monstrous usurpation of power was much increased by the following circumstance, that the Commissioners were expresly authorized, by their Commissions, to "erect *Gallowes* or *Gibbetts*, and *in such places as they* "*shall think fit!*"

lish Legiflature,) we muft neceffarily exclude, from the prefent enquiry, the moft diftant idea that Mr. Barrington's 2d Precedent, *for taxing Ireland by Prerogative*, can poffibly afford the leaft evidence againft the *juft Rights* of the Subjects in *Ireland*; for, if *fuch Precedents* are admitted to prove any thing at all, they prove too much; for they equally "fhew that it was *then imagined the King could tax*" and opprefs *even England itfelf*, as well as "*Ireland*, by his Prero-"gative, without *the intervention of* "*Parliament*;" and I am very fure that the worthy writer, who unguardedly cited from Rymer the above-mentioned Precedent againft *Ireland*, would be as zealous to oppofe any fuch doctrine as myfelf.

His 3d Precedent is ftill more deftitute, if poffible, of legal evidence. — 'What would have been the anfwer of

'the

'the *Engliſh Legiſlature*, (ſays he,) in 'the year 1650, to the late claim of 'Independency in the Colonies, will 'appear by the preamble to an Ordi-'nance of the 3d Oct. of that year:' — "Whereas in Virginia, and the iſlands "of St. Chriſtopher's, Nevis, Montſerrat, "and divers other iſlands and places in "America, which were planted at the "coſt, and ſettled by the people and "authority, of this nation, which are "and ought to be ſubordinate to, and "dependent upon, *England*, and hath "ever ſince the planting thereof, and "ought to be ſubject to ſuch Laws, Or-"ders, and Regulations, as *ſhall be* "*made by the Parliament of England*;" p. 146.

But, though this was indeed the opinion of what Mr. Barrington calls "*the* "*Engliſh Legiſlature* in the year 1650," yet no juſt argument can be drawn from thence

thence with respect to the present question, (*viz.* the pretension to bind Ireland without *Representation* or *Assent*;) because it affords as good an argument, as the others above-mentioned, for binding even *England* itself, *without any Representation or Assent at all*, since the *said Legislature* (as it is called) was totally defective in every point that is essentially necessary to constitute an *English Legislature*; for (besides the total suppression of the legal Rights of the Crown to a Share in the Legislature) even the necessary *Assent* of the whole body of the *People* was also excluded, since it is evident that neither the Lords nor the Commons of England were represented in that packed junto of Hypocrites which was *then* called the "*English Legislature!*" for, after the violent seizure of 41 Members of the House of Commons (38) by the Army, on

(38) In Rushworth's Collection, 4th part, vol. 2, p. 1355, we read the names of the Members imprisoned

on the 6th of December, 1648, and the forcible exclusion of about 100 more, (39) by the same unlawful power, on the following day, (preparatory to the illegal trial and murder of the King in 1648-9,) the Long-Parliament no longer *represented the nation*, but was merely the Representative of a most dangerous *standing Army*; for such the national Militia was then become; the several individuals thereof having, by a constant military

soned by the Army, which were inserted in "*the Proposals and Desires of the Army*," presented that day to the Parliament by Colonel Whaley and other officers; and in Mr. Rushworth's Diary for the next day, Dec. 7, we find the following Memorandum relating to that transaction: *viz.* "The Members seized on by *the Army* were this day removed from Mr. Duke's house, "(commonly called *Hell,*) in Westminster, WHERE "THEY WERE ALL LAST NIGHT, to two inns in "the Strand, *viz.* the King's-Head and the Swan, "and there *have a guard upon them*;" p. 1356.

(39) "Le 7 de Decembre les Membres des Communes, en se rendant à leur Chambre, y trouverent "à la porte en dehors et en dedans une garde qui en "empêcha *un grand nombre* d'entrer. Le Comte de "Clarendon dit qu'il *y* en eut *environ cent* à qui on "refusa l'entrée." Rapin, tom. 8, liv. 21, p. 707.

litary Service for a few Years (40) (*viz.* from four to ſix Years) acquired a fixt diſlike and contempt for thoſe uſeful employments by which they were formerly enabled (whilſt a mere militia) to earn their bread, ſo that they now acknowledged no profeſſion but that of *arms*, and conſequently were now become a *regular ſtanding army* of mercenaries, with a ſeparate intereſt of their own from the reſt of the nation (41);

U and

(40) The orders of the Lords and Commons for raiſing the militia to oppoſe the King's commiſſions of array were dated in 1642. See Ruſhworth's Collection, part 3. vol. 1. p. 678, 679, 684, 685, 689, and 765.

(41) " —— Les officiers et les ſoldats comprenoient bien qu'on vouloit ſe defaire d'eux," (that is, the war being at an end, the Parliament was inclined to reduce the number of regular troops by degrees,) " et que la plûpart n'etoient gueres en état d'aller " reprendre leur profeſſions, après avoir été quatre ou " cinq ans occupez à faire la guerre. Il y avoit dans " l'armée un grand nombre *d' officiers* qui n' é- " toient avant la guerre que *des artiſans* et qui ne " voyoient qu' avec peine qu'ils alloient être reduits à

" quitter

and a *ſtanding army*, by whomſoever paid, muſt ever be dangerous to conſtitutional Liberty and Law.

The army were, indeed, the *nominal* ſervants of the Parliament, but were nevertheleſs the abſolute Lords and ſovereign Directors of the ſame, having ejected whomſoever they thought proper, and thereby modelled the *national Repreſentative* into a repreſentation only of their own body and party, (as has been ſaid,) ſo that it ceaſed from that time to deſerve the Name of a *Parliament* or "*Legiſlature*,"

" quitter leur emplois qui leur donnoient de l'auto-
" rité, et à reprendre *leurs anciens métiers* pour ſe mê-
" ler, comme auparavant, dans la foule du petit peu-
" ple. Ces gens là, le même que ceux que les indepen-
" dans avoient attirez dans leur parti, étoient diſpo-
" ſez à tout entreprendre, pour n'être pas obligez à
" changer la manière de vie qu'ils avoient menée de-
" puis quelques années. Cromwell donc, et les offi-
" ciers de ſon parti, profitant de cette diſpoſition,
" s'attachèrent à inſpirer à l'armée un eſprit de me-
" contentement *contre les deux chambres*, en quoi ils ne
" réuſſirent que trop bien. Rapin, Tom. VIII. p. 579.

" *Legislature*," being a mere tool of military power, which was permitted to sit for no other purpose than that of lending a pretended *parliamentary Authority* to the arbitrary measures and wicked resolutions of an illegal Council of War; as if the mere *Name* of a *Parliament* without the thing itself (a due Representation of the people) was sufficient to authorize and justify the most detestable Despotism! The whole proceedings of the Council of War, from the time the King was seized at Holmby, (though he himself was deceived by their temporizing dissimulation,) clearly proves their fixed intention to proceed to extremities, contrary to the declared sentiments (42) of

(42) See the Votes of the Commons on the 28th of April, 1648, *viz.* " 1. That the Government of " the Kingdom should be still by King, Lords, and " Commons. 2. That the ground-work for this Go- " vernment should be the propositions last presented to " the King at Hampton-Court; and, 3dly, That any " Member of the House shall have leave to speak free- " ly

of the former Parliament, as well as of the citizens of *London* (43) in general, and of

" ly to any Votes, Ordinances, or Declarations, con- " cerning the *King*," &c. Rushworth's Collect. part 4. vol. 2. p. 1074.

Tuesday *June* 27, 1648.

(43) "This day a Petition from the Lord Mayor, Al- " dermen, and Common Council of the City of *London* " was presented to both Houses of Parliament; the sub- " stance thereof, for satisfaction of those that have not " seen the Petition, take briefly thus:——That a per- " sonal treaty may be obtained betwixt his Majesty " and both Houses, *in the City of London*, or some other " convenient place, where it may be most for *the ho- " nour of his Majesty's royal person*, and *preservation of " the Parliament*, as their honours thought fit; unto " which treaty they humbly desire our brethren of " *Scotland* may be invited; that so according to *the " duty of our allegiance*, protestation, solemn league, " and Covenant, *his Majesty's royal person, honour, and " estate, may be preserved*; the *power and privilege of " Parliament maintained*; *the just Rights and Liberties of " the Subjects restored*; Religion and Government of " the Church in purity established; all differences " may be the better composed, and a firm and lasting " peace concluded; and the union between the two " Kingdoms continued, according to the covenant; " ALL ARMIES DISBANDED; and all your soldiers " just arrears satisfied; the Kingdom's burthens eased, " and the laudable Government thereof, by the good " and

of almoſt the whole preſbyterian party, (including at that time a very great majority of the people,) who were earneſtly deſirous to maintain the ancient conſtitution of State, by reſtoring the King to ſuch a ſhare of *limited Power* as they thought conſiſtent with their own ſafety: But, alas! the *ſtanding Army* was now become *the ruling Sovereign* of the Kingdom, and was not leſs zealous to maintain an *unlimited* Authority than the former ruling *Sovereign*, whom they had ſo lately fought againſt and impriſoned for the like unlawful pretenſions; ſo that the arbitrary proceedings and injuſtice of the King, in the beginning of his Reign, were *ſeverely repaid in kind* by proceedings equally arbitrary, illegal, and unjuſt; as *Oppreſſion*

" and wholeſome Laws and Cuſtoms, happily ad-" vanced." For this, both Lords and Commons, reſpectively, thank the petitioners for their good affection to the Parliament, and ſignify their concurrence in the ſame ſentiments. Ruſhworth, part 4. vol. 2. p. 1167, and 1168.

preſſion is generally puniſhed by *Oppreſſion*, that even the *injuſtice* of mankind may demonſtrate the *juſtice* of an all-ruling Providence in the Government of the World!

This mock Parliament, ſupported by the *ſtanding Army*, held the nation in ſlavery (44) from December, 1648, to April, 1653, including the year referred to, as above, for the ſenſe of the then "*Engliſh Legiſlature*" concerning the authority of Parliament over Virginia and the other Colonies.

In the beginning of 1653, the artful Cromwell found himſelf ſo well eſtabliſhed in his military poſt of *General*, or *Imperator*, of the ſtanding Army, (for ſuch is the original root both of the name and power of *Emperors*,) that he ventured,

(44) "J'ai déja dit, que le Parliament n' avoit d' autre appui *que l' Armée*. C' étoit par le *moyen de l' Armée* qu'il tenoit la nation dans *la ſervitude*." Rapin, tom. 9. p. 57.

tured, by dint of his *military authority*, to turn the despicable mock *Legislature* out of the Parliament-House (45), and, by the same redoubtable authority, chose another junto, consisting of 144 Members, *without consulting the Nation at all*, that the new *nominal* Parliament might be still more obedient in *representing* and fulfilling

(45) Cromwell, —— "après avoir concerté toutes " choses avec les *principaux officiers*, se rendit au Parliament le $\frac{20}{30}$ Avril, accompagné d'un petit nombre *d'officiers et de soldats*, et sans autre préambule il dit " aux Membres du Parliament, qu'il venoit mettre fin à " leur autorité dont ils avoient fait un mauvais usage, " et, que sans deliberer, ils eussent à se dissoudre sur le " champ. En même temps *les officiers et les soldats* " entrèrent, et se tinrent à la porte, pendant que les " Membres se retiroient hors de la Chambre. A mesure qu'ils sortoient, Cromwell disoit à l'un, qu'il " étoit un yvrogne, à un autre, qu'il etoit un voleur, " sans en epargner aucun de ceux qu'il connoissoit " pour ses ennemis. Ensuite, il donna à garder la " Masse, qu'on porte devant l'Orateur, à un de ses " Officiers, et ferma les portes à la clef. Cette action " étoit *extraordinaire*, mais elle ne l' étoit pas plus " que celle que *le General Fairfax* avoit fait peu " d'années auparavant, lors qu'il avoit fait *chasser de la* " *Chambre et emprisonner les Membres* QUI N'ETOIENT " PAS AGREABLES à l'Armée." Ibid. p. 59.

fulfilling the *Will* and *Pleasure* of its *military* Constituents: This wretched Assembly, though in the highest degree despicable in itself, was nevertheless invested with *sovereign* AUTHORITY (46) over *England*, *Scotland*, and *Ireland*, by an instrument drawn up expressly for *that purpose*, and signed by the *General* (Cromwell) and *the principal Officers of the Army*; so that we have here an undeniable precedent for governing *England*, *Scotland*, and *Ireland*, without the *Representation* and *Assent* of the *People* of any of these Kingdoms; and yet no one will pretend to say, that the same can justify any future attempts to deprive either

(46) "Ces nouveaux *Souverains* s'étant assemblez au "jour marqué, Cromwell les harangua, et, après avoir "fini son discours, il leur delivra un instrument en "parchemin, signé par lui même et par *les principaux* "*officiers* de l' Armée, par lequel on leur deféroit *l' Autorité Souveraine*. Cet ecrit portoit, que *tous les Sujets d' Angleterre, d' Ecosse, et d' Irlande*, étoient tenus "de leur obéir, jusqu'au 3-13 de Novembre de "l'année suivante 1654, c'est à dire pendant un an et "quatre mois," &c. Ibid. 61.

either the people of England, Scotland, or even of *Ireland*, of their just right to a free and frequent *Representation* in Parliament. Now, " *the English Legislature*" of 1653, (for the Title is not less due than it was in 1650,) having continued their sittings for about five months, dissolved themselves, and returned the instrument of their *Sovereignty* to the *General* and his *military Council*. (47) And, two days afterwards, the *Council of Officers*, by virtue of this devolved authority, which the sham Parliament (of their own creating and appointing) had re-delivered into their hands, were pleased to declare, that, for the future, the *Government of the Republick* (48) (plainly meaning, as appears

(47) On the $\frac{12}{22}$ of December, 1653. Ibid. p. 63.

(48) " Deux jours après, *le Conseil des Officiers*, en " vertu de l'autorité que le précédent Parlement" (meaning the junto of 144 persons, *constituted and chosen merely by the General, or by the Army*) " venoit de lui " deferer, declara, qu'à l'avenir, LE GOVERNEMENT " DE

appears by the event, not only the ſovereign *executive* Power, but alſo the full and ſupreme *legiſlative* Power of the Republic, or three united Kingdoms, for a certain time) (49) ſhould *reſide* in *one ſingle perſon*, namely, their own *military Commander*, *General Cromwell*, whom they inveſted with the title and power of Protector of the three Kingdoms. I have thus far purſued the hiſtory of thoſe arbitrary times, as well to ſhew the danger of keeping a *ſtanding Army*,

" DE LA REPUBLIQUE *reſideroit* DANS UNE SEULE " PERSONNE, ſavoir, dans celle d'Olivier Cromwell, " *General des Armées* d'Angleterre, d'Ecoſſe, et d'Irlande; et qu'il auroit le titre de *Protecteur des trois* " *Royaumes*, et qu'il ſeroit aſſiſté d'un conſeil de 21 " perſonnes." Rapin, Tome ix. p. 64.

(49) *Viz.* from the $\frac{16}{26}$ Dec. 1653, to the $\frac{3}{13}$ Sept. 1654, as appears by the 1ſt and 8th Articles of what this *military* Council were pleaſed to call "*an Act of* "*Government*," thereby proving their own uſurpation of the *ſupreme legiſlative Authority*; which Authority they were afterwards pleaſed to lodge in the *ſingle perſon* of their *General*, by the 7th and 8th Articles of the ſaid "*Act of Government*." Ibid. p. 64.

my, (50) and of permitting a *national Militia* to become ſuch, (51) as to de-

X 2 monſtrate

(50) I might have ſaved myſelf much trouble, upon this point, had I been aware, when I wrote the foregoing pages, that the danger of keeping *ſtanding Armies* had been ſo well enforced by Mr. Quincy, in his Obſervations on the Boſton Port Bill. That ingenious and ſenſible Writer has very judiciouſly collected a number of unqueſtionable examples upon the ſubject, which, together with his own pertinent obſervations upon them, demand the moſt ſerious attention not only of every *loyal* Engliſh Subject, at this time, but of all friends to mankind in general.

(51) The example of military Tyranny, which I have already recited, demonſtrates the great danger of permitting any part of a *national Militia* to be abſent, longer than is abſolutely neceſſary, from the particular *county* or *diſtrict* to which it properly belongs; for, as ſoon as *Militia-Men* begin to depend upon their *Pay*, or "*Solde*," * inſtead of their *induſtry* and the regular daily employments which they followed at home, they ceaſe to be the conſtitutional defenders of their country, and become mere *Soldiers* ("*Soldats*") or Mercenaries: and therefore, as it is now reported that great pains are, at this time, taken, in the ſeveral American Colonies, to renew the ancient diſcipline of the *Militia*, in their reſpective provinces, it is a matter of great conſequence, (as well for their own *internal* happineſs and liberty, as for the preſervation of peace and union with

* "*Dictionnaire militaire*," p. 417.

monſtrate the inſufficiency and *illegality* of the *Precedents* which have been cited to juſtify the fatal *pretenſion* of England to govern *Ireland*, and the other Colonies, without the *Repreſentation* and *Aſſent* of the reſpective inhabitants; for we might as well enquire "what would "have been the anſwer of the *Engliſh* "*Legiſlature* in the year 1653," (when the *whole Legiſlature* was compriſed within the narrow compaſs of Cromwell's own

with the mother-country, and a continuance of that due conſtitutional ſubjection, to *the Crown of Great-Britain*, which is the true intereſt of all parties, as it connects every branch of the empire, and inſures *mutual* confidence and protection againſt *foreign* enemies,) that no perſons whatever be allowed the rank of *Officers*, in any of their provincial Regiments of *Militia*, unleſs they have a competent fortune, either in *Land* or Money, to enable them to live comfortably, without military pay, leſt they ſhould ever entertain a *ſeparate Intereſt* from that of the Public, and, like the degenerate *Militia* under Cromwell, *enſlave* their country! Even a *common Militia-Man* is not properly qualified for that *public Truſt* (for ſuch it is) unleſs, from his ſituation in life, or as the maſter of a family, he has ſome permanent intereſt in the welfare of the community.

own doublet,) as "*in the year* 1650," to which this learned writer has referred us; ſince the authority of the *nominal* Legiſlature in 1650 was entirely *illegal*, as well as that in 1653, both of them having been ſet up and maintained by the ſame unconſtitutional arbitrary power; and both of them totally void of the indiſpenſable *Repreſentation* of the people: for though the wretched remains of the Long-Parliament in 1650 (being about 80 Repreſentatives or Members, inſtead of 513 that had been elected (52) at the beginning of that Parliament)

(52) "Ainſi ce Parlement, qui dans ſon commence-
" ment avoit été compoſé du Roi, d'une Chambre d'en-
" viron ſix-vingts Seigneurs, et d'une Chambre des
" Communes, où il y avoit *cinq cens treize Députez*, ſe vit
" reduit à une Chambre des Communes compoſée d'*en-*
" *viron quatre-vingts Membres*, dont il y en avoit très peu
" qui, au commencement de ce Parlement, euſſent
" cinq-cens livres ſterling de rente. Cependant ces
" membres, quoiqu'en ſi petit nombre, s'attribuoient
" le *nom de Parliament*, et agiſſoit comme ayant réuni,
" dans leur corps, le pouvoir qui avoit auparavant
" reſidé dans le Roi, dans les Seigneurs, et dans les
" Communes. Cela pourroit paroître fort étrange,
" ſi

liament) were indeed chosen by a small part of the people of England, yet the legal *Representation*, even of that small part, was *out of date* and void, from the length of time that the said Representatives had continued without Re-election, which was about ten years; whereas it is well known that the due effect, or *virtue*, of popular *Representation*, was formerly supposed to be incapable (like some *annual* fruits) of being so long preserved in useful purity, without *a seasonable renewal*, (53) from time to time; so

" si on n'étoit pas déja informé *de ce qui s'étoit passé*, " *et de la terreur que* L'ARMÉE *inspiroit à tout le* " *monde*." Rapin, tome ix. p. 4.

(53) The sensible and patriotic author of the "Letters from a Farmer in Pennsylvania to the Inhabitants of the British Colonies (1774)," remarks, in a note on page 103, that, "the last *Irish* Parliament continued *thirty-three years*, that is," (says he,) "during all the late reign. The present Parliament there has continued from the beginning of this reign, and probably will continue" (says he) "to the end!"

This is indeed, as he justly calls it, a most "*pernicious particularity*," it being a greater defect in the constitutional

ſo that our more prudent Anceſtors (imitating nature) required alſo an *annual* (54) renewal

conſtitutional Liberties of *Ireland* than any other that I ever heard of; and, as it is apparently contrary to the intention and legal conſtitution of Parliaments, muſt neceſſarily reflect the greateſt diſhonour on thoſe perſons, whoever they are, that have introduced this monſtrous infringement on the natural Rights of the *Iriſh* Subjects.

Theſe excellent Letters, which contain much ſeaſonable inſtruction, are ſaid to be written by John Dickinſon, Eſq. the ſame eminent Author to whom thanks were moſt deſervedly given, by the Committee for the Province of Penſylvania, on the 21ſt of July laſt, "for the great aſſiſtance they had derived from the "application of his eminent abilities to the ſervice of "his country, in" (another) "performance," ſince publiſhed, intitled, "A new Eſſay" (by the Pennſylvanian Farmer) "on the conſtitutional Power of "Great-Britain over the Colonies in America," *&c.* And the ſaid Committee, with great juſtice and propriety, recommended that performance, "as highly "deſerving the peruſal and ſerious conſideration of "every friend of liberty," *&c.*

(54) Sir Edw. Coke, in his 4th Inſt. p. 9, ſpeaking of "the matters of Parliament," informs us of the reaſons uſually expreſſed in the writs for calling a new Parliament; as "pro quibuſdam arduis urgentibus ne-"gotiis, nos ſtatum, et defenſionem regni noſtri Angliæ, "et Eccleſiæ Anglicanæ concernentibus quoddam parlia-"mentum noſtrum, *&c.* teneri ordinavimus," *&c.* And he adds,

renewal of their *parliamentary Represen-tation*, as being neceſſary for the mainte-nance of public virtue.

Thus

adds, in the next paragraph, " Now, for as much" (ſays he) " as divers Laws and Statutes have been " enacted and provided for theſe ends aforeſaid, and " that divers miſchiefs in particular, and divers grie-" vances in general, concerning the honour and ſafety " of the King, the State, and defence of the King-" dome, and of the Church of England, might be " prevented, *an excellent Law* was made, anno 36 " Edw. III. c. 10. which, *being applied to the ſaid* " *Writs of Parliament*, doth, in a few and effectual " words, ſet down the true ſubject of a Parliament in " theſe words : *For the maintenance of the ſaid articles* " *and ſtatutes, and redreſs of divers miſchiefs and grie-* " *vances, which daily happen*, A PARLIAMENT SHALL " BE HOLDEN EVERY YEAR, as another time was " ordained by a ſtatute." Which Statute, here referred to, was made in the 4th year of the ſame reign, cap 14. " Item, it is accorded, that a Parliament ſhall be hol-" den EVERY YEAR ONCE, *and more often if need be*." But Sir William Blackſtone ſuppoſes that the King never was " obliged, by theſe Statutes, to call a *new* Parlia-" ment *every year* ; but only to permit a Parliament to " ſit annually for the redreſs of grievances, and diſ-" patch of buſineſs, *if need be*." (1 Com. c. 2, p. 153.)

It is too true, indeed, that our Kings, in general, did not think themſelves " *obliged*, by theſe Statutes," (as they ought in conſcience to have been, for the ſafety

of

Thus the third Example, given by this learned gentleman, for taxing *Ireland* and *Virginia*, &c. without the assent of

Y the

of their souls,) "to call *a new Parliament every year*:" nay, it is certain that many of them would never have called a Parliament at all, had they not been "*obliged*" by necessity and the circumstances of the times. But by what authority could a representative in one Parliament take his seat in the *next annual Parliament*, without *re-election*, before any laws were made for lengthening the duration of Parliaments? And besides, if the King did "*only permit* a Parliament to sit annually," &c. by what authority could the Parliament be convened at all, under such a circumstance, seeing that a *mere permission to sit* excludes the idea of a prorogation from year to year? However, the learned Commentator himself very justly observes, in a preceding page, (150,) concerning "the manner and time of assembling" that the "Parliament is regularly to be summoned by the "King's *Writ* or Letter, issued out of Chancery." And it is well known that these Writs are not addressed to the knights, citizens, and burgesses, elected for any *former* Parliament, but to *the Sheriffs alone*, to cause *Knights, Citizens, &c. to be elected*; for, when the said Acts were made, such an absurdity in politics had never been conceived in England, as that of entrusting the *Representation* of the people, for *a term of years*, (as at present,) to the persons elected! On the contrary, when the business of each Sessions was finished, the Parliament, of course, was at an end; and therefore Lord Coke did not speak in vain, when he mentioned "*the*

"*excellent*

the reſpective inhabitants, is manifeſtly *illegal*; ſince it muſt appear, that what

" *excellent Law*" (*viz.* the Act for *annual* Parliaments) " *being applied to the ſaid Writs of Parliament*," &c. before recited.

A man of ſo much good-ſenſe, learning, and judgement, as Sir William Blackſtone is maſter of, muſt be well aware of the pernicious effects of inveſting the Repreſentatives of the people with a legiſlative power, beyond the conſtitutional term of A SINGLE SESSION, without *Re-election*; and therefore I cannot but be ſurprized at the unguarded manner in which he has expreſſed himſelf in his Comment on the two *excellent Statutes* of Edward III. for *annual* Parliaments; *viz.* that the King is not, " or ever was, obliged by theſe " Statutes to call a *new* Parliament every year," *&c.* He has cauſed the word *new* to be printed in *Italics*, as if he meant thereby to inſinuate, that the Legiſlatures of thoſe early times were not unacquainted with our modern idea of conferring on the popular Repreſentatives a kind of *continued ſenatorial dignity*, without *Re-election*, for ſeveral years together; whereas he certainly muſt have known that this corrupt *modern* practice has produced a *new order* of men amongſt us, a moſt dangerous increaſe of ariſtocratical power, which was entirely unknown to our Anceſtors in the glorious reign of Edward III. If he could ſhew that there *ever* was a Parliament, in thoſe times, that was *not a* NEW *Parliament*, his Comment might be juſtified! But it is notorious that Writs were iſſued to the Sheriffs, for *new* Elections, almoſt *every year* during that whole reign: The Writs, for the moſt part, are

what he calls "*the English Legislature*, "in the year 1650," was totally void of

Y 2 every

are still preserved with the Returns upon them. In the catalogue of Election-Writs, which Prynn has given in his *Brevia Parliamentaria Rediviva*, p. 4 to 6, there is an account of Writs issued for *new* Elections in every year of that King's reign, between his 34th (when the last Act for annual Parliaments was made) and his 50th year, except 3, *viz.* the 40th, 41st, and 48th years; in which years the Records of Summons to the Prelates and Lords of Parliament are also wanting, as appears by Sir William Dugdale's "perfect Copy of Summons to Parliament, of the Nobility," &c.

And yet this affords no absolute proof that Parliaments were not held *in those very years* for which the Writs are wanting; because the bundles of Writs for the said years may have been lost or mislaid. The only wonder is, that more have not been absolutely lost, when we consider the very little care that had been taken of them; for Prynne found many of these Writs dispersed amongst a vast miscellaneous heap of other records on various subjects, (as he himself relates in his Epistle-Dedicatory to King Charles II. of his *Brevia Parliamentaria Rediviva,*) calling the said heap a "*confused Chaos*, under corroding, putrifying cobwebs, dust, and filth, in the darkest corner of Cæsar's Chapel in the White Tower, as *mere useless Reliques not worthy to be calendred*," &c. And, in page 103 of that same work, he speaks of 117 Bundles of Writs, whereof 97 had only been then *lately* discovered, filed, and bundled, by himself: "But many of these 117 Bundles" (says he) "are

" *not*

every eſſential and legal qualification to render it worthy of ſo diſtinguiſhing a title:

" *not compleat*, above half or three parts of the Writs " being either rotted, conſumed, maymed, torn, or " *utterly loſt*, through careleſſneſs, wet, cankers, or " other caſualties; and ſome of them have not above " two, three, or four Writs, and one or two but one " Writ and Retorn remaining."

But that there were really Writs for Parliaments, even in theſe *three* years, which appear to be wanting, at leaſt in *two* of them, is very certain; becauſe it was in the 40th year of this reign, as Sir Edward Coke informs us, (4 Inſt. p. 13,) that the Pope demanded homage for the kingdoms of England and Ireland, and the arrears of revenue granted by King John to Pope Innocent III. " whereupon the King, in the *ſame year*, " *calleth his Court of Parliament*,"* &c. as Sir Edward Coke proves from the Parliament-Rolls of that year, N°. 8, remarking, at the ſame time, that the Act then made was " never yet printed." See the margin, 4th Inſt. p. 13.

And

* In this Parliament it was unanimouſly agreed, by the Prelates, Dukes, Counts, Barons, and the *Commons*, (" et *la Commun*," and again, " *et Communes*,") " that the ſaid King John, nor no other, " could put himſelf, nor his Realm, nor his People, in ſuch Subjec- " tion, without *their Aſſent*, (' ſans aſſent de eux;') and, if it was " done, it was done without their Aſſent," (that is, without the Aſſent of the *Commons*, for the Aſſent of the Barons was expreſſed in the Charter,) " and contrary to his Oath at his Coronation." P. 14. Whereupon Lord Coke remarks, in the margin, that " no King can " put himſelf, nor his Realm, nor his People, in ſuch Subjection, " without Aſſent of the *Lords and Commons in Parliament*," *&c.*

title: but, ſuppoſing that "the Engliſh "Legiſlature, in the year 1650," had been

And it appears that a Parliament was held alſo in the 48th year of this reign, becauſe ſupplies were in that year granted to the King by Parliament, as related by Sir Richard Baker, in his Chronicle, p. 173, *viz.* "*in his eight and fortieth year,* IN A PARLIAMENT, is granted him a 10th of the Clergy, and a "15th of the Laity." So that there is but *one* year, out of ſo many, in which we cannot trace the meeting of the annual Parliaments: And annual Writs for *new* Elections were regularly iſſued for the firſt 18 years of the following reign, (as appears by Prynn's "2d "part of a brief Regiſter and Survey of the ſeveral "kinds and forms of parliamentary Writs,"* pages 116 and 117,) till Richard II. (that wretched perjured monarch) had rendered himſelf *abſolute.*†

After conſidering theſe unqueſtionable evidences of the iſſuing Writs *annually* for *new* Elections, it will be difficult to comprehend the meaning of Sir William Blackſtone's Comment on the ſaid two Acts for *annual* Parliaments: "Not that he (the King) is, or ever "was, obliged by theſe Statutes to call a *new* Parlia-"ment every year; but only to permit a Parliament "to ſit annually for the redreſs of grievances and "diſpatch of buſineſs, *if need be.* — Theſe laſt words" (ſays

† His arbitrary proceedings very ſoon afterwards occaſioned his own loſs of Power, and total Ejectment from the Throne; ſo that, notwithſtanding his boaſted *Firmneſs* in executing his favourite Meaſures, he was at laſt reduced to the moſt abject acknowledgements of his own unworthineſs to reign.

been a legal and conſtitutional Parliament, yet the Reſolutions he has mentioned

(ſays he) " are ſo *looſe and vague*, that ſuch of our mo-" narchs as were enclined to govern without Parlia-" ments, neglected the convoking them, ſometimes for " a very conſiderable period, under pretence that there " *was no need of them*," &c.

But " *theſe laſt words*" are not *ſo looſe and vague* as either to juſtify his own explanation of the ſaid Statutes, (*viz.* not " to call a *new* Parliament every year, " but only to *permit* a Parliament to ſit," *&c.*) or to excuſe, in the leaſt degree, the criminal neglects of thoſe depraved monarchs who were inclined to govern without them: for the words, " *if need be*," cannot, according to the moſt obvious ſenſe of the Act wherein they are found, be applied to the main purpoſe of the Act, (the holding *annual Parliaments,*) but merely to the remaining part of the ſentence, *viz.* " *and more* " *often*:" that is, " and more often, if need be." The Order, " *that a Parliament ſhall be holden* EVERY " YEAR ONCE," is abſolute, and the diſcretionary power, expreſſed in the words " *if need be*," relates apparently to the calling Parliaments " *more often*:" for, if the ſaid diſcretionary words, " *if need be*," could, with any propriety, be applied to the whole ſentence, the Act itſelf would have been nugatory; which could never be the *intention* of the Legiſlature: but the true meaning and ſenſe of the Legiſlature is very clearly proved by the hiſtories of thoſe times: for it is manifeſt, not only that *new* Repreſentatives were elected *every year* (with only one exception) for

a

tioned would have been totally *illegal*, and amount to no more than a mere vain assertion,

a considerable number of years after the last of the said Acts was made, (which confirms the main purpose of the Acts, *viz.* the holding *annual Parliaments*,) but it is also manifest, that Parliaments were frequently held "*more often*" than once a year; ‡ which amply confirms also what I have before said, concerning the meaning of the discretionary power, expressed in the said Act, by the words "*if need be.*"

These very frequent Elections (sometimes two, three, and four, times IN ONE YEAR) sufficiently prove that the power, delegated by the people to their Representatives, continued no longer in force than during the Session of the particular Parliament to which they were summoned; which being "*once determined,*" (says Prynne, 1st part of Brief Register, *&c.* of Parl. Writs, p. 334.) "*they presently ceased to be Knights, Citizens, Burgesses, Barons, in any succeeding Parliaments or Councils, unless newly elected and retorned to serve in them, by the King's* NEW *Writs, as our Law-Books*" (referring to 4 Ed. IV. *f.* 44. Brook, Officer, 25. 34 Hen. VIII. c. 24.) "*and experience resolve,*" &c. And therefore Judge Blackstone's insinuation, against the calling of a *new* Parliament, has no real foundation: for, if it was the intention of the Legislature,

‡ Writs were issued for electing 3 *new* Parliaments in the 6th year of Edw. III. 2 in his 11th year, 3 in his 12th year, and even 4 in his 14th year; and there appear to have been 2 *new* Parliaments in the 7th of R. II. See *Prynne's Brevia Parliamentaria Rediviva*, p. 5 & 6.

assertion, as void of *Law* and *Reason* as it was really of *Effect*; which is proved by

Legislature, in the two Acts abovementioned, that the King should ever summon *any Parliament at all*, they must necessarily be understood to mean a *new* Parliament on all occasions; *i. e.* not only that the regular Parliaments, which they ordained "*to be* holden every *year* "*once*," should be *new* Parliaments, but those also that should be summoned upon any extraordinary unforeseen occasions; which is sufficiently expressed in the 1st of the said Acts, by the words, "*and more often*, "*if need be*." The meaning of the Act is *unquestionably* proved by the actual issuing of writs, to the Sheriffs, for electing Knights, Citizens, *&c.* for *two*, *three*, and sometimes *four new* Parliaments, *in one year*, as mentioned above: And if any person should object, that such *very frequent Elections* must be attended with insuperable difficulties and inconveniences, we may quote the experience of all ancient times, as affording ample and sufficient proofs to the contrary; "there being not above two or three cases of elections "questioned, or complained of, from 49 Hen. III. "till 22 Edw. IV." (that is, more than 200 years,) "for ought that appears by the Retornes or Parlia- "ment-Rolls, and NOT SO MUCH AS ONE DOUBLE "RETORNE OR INDENTURE, wherewith all the *late* "Bundles, or Writs, are stored, and the House of "Commons and *late* Committees of Privileges pes- "tered, perplexed, to the *great retarding* of the "more weighty public affairs of the King and King- "dom." Prynne, Brevia Parl. Rediv. p. 137. This enormous

by " *the* ANSWER *of the Engliſh Legiſla-* " *ture,*" *at Virginia,* (then repreſenting

Z *the*

enormous evil, the retardment of buſineſs, by undue Returns, will not (I may venture, without the ſpirit of prophecy, to aſſert) be remedied by the *new Regulation* for that purpoſe. The Commons were never (in ancient times of Freedom) eſteemed the proper Judges of their own Elections, but the *King* alone, that is, in his *limited* judicial capacity, by his Juſtices and his ſworn Juries, in the Courts of Common-Law. If my countrymen will ſeriouſly conſider all theſe points, they muſt be convinced that the only ſure method of healing the alarming diſtempers of our political Conſtitution* is to reſtore to the people their ancient and juſt Right to elect a *new* Parliament, " *every year once,* and *more often if need be,*" whatſoever Judge Blackſtone may think of it!

No Parliament could have any right to deprive the people of this ineſtimable Law, unleſs the Repreſentatives had expreſsly conſulted their reſpective conſtituents upon it; as the alteration was of too much moment to be intruſted to the diſcretion of any *Repreſentatives* or *Deputies* whatſoever, being infinitely more important than " *any new device,* moved on the King's " behalf,

* *Viz.* the enormous national Debt; the numerous Penſions; the ſecret parliamentary Influence; a ſtanding Army of near 100 Battalions of Foot, beſides Cavalry, in time of Peace! *&c. &c. &c.* which muſt render the *Eſtates* and *Property* of individuals precarious and inſecure, or finally EAT THEM UP with *growing burthens,* if theſe fatal ſymptoms of the moſt dangerous *political conſumption* are not ſpeedily checked and thrown off, by the wholeſome preſcriptions of a *free and equal Repreſentation of* THE PEOPLE.

the People of that province,) to the unreasonable pretensions, beforementioned, of the *mock Legislature* at London; for otherwise,

" behalf, in Parliament, *for his aid, or the like*;" for the most essential and fundamental Right of the *whole body of the Commons* (I mean the *Principals*, not the *Deputies* or *Agents)* was materially injured by the fatal change, and the people's power of controul, for the general good of the kingdom, was thereby apparently diminished! so that, if it is the duty of Representatives (even in " *any new device*" of mere " *aid, or* " *the like*") to consult their Constituents, how much more, upon the proposal of so material an alteration in the Constitution, ought they to have answered, that, " *in this new device, they* DARE NOT AGREE " WITHOUT CONFERENCE WITH THEIR " COUNTRIES!" These are the words of Lord Coke, who mentions them as the proper answer, " *when any* " *new device is moved*," &c. and he adds, " whereby " it appeareth" (says he) " that SUCH CONFERENCE " *is warrantable by the Law and Custome of Parliament*," 4 Inst. p. 14; so that no *Representative* can be justified (according to " *the Law and Custome of Parliament*") who refuses to receive the Instructions of his Constituents, notwithstanding that several very sensible, worthy, and (I believe) sincerely patriotic gentlemen have lately declared themselves to be of *a contrary opinion*; but, when they peruse the several authorities which I have cited, concerning the absolute necessity of *a very frequent appeal* to the sense of *the whole body of the people*, I trust, in their candour and love of truth, that they will alter their sentiments.

otherwiſe, if we were to conſider " *what* " *would have been* THE ANSWER" (or rather what *really were* THE CLAIMS) of the *one Legiſlature*, without conſidering, at the ſame time, the *real* ANSWER of *the other*, to ſuch *vain* and *unjuſt* pretenſions, we ſhould lay ourſelves open to the charge of *partiality!*

The judicious Author of a late " Appeal to the Juſtice and Intereſts of the " People of Great-Britain, in the preſent " Diſputes with America," has reported the Anſwer of the *Virginian Legiſlature* on that occaſion. " Upon the diſſolu- " tion of the Monarchy," (ſays he,) " the Commonwealth diſpatched a Go- " vernor, WITH A SQUADRON, to take " poſſeſſion of Virginia. He was *per-* " *mitted* to land, *upon Articles*, of which " the following is one, and *deciſively* " *ſhews what were their original ideas of* " *their Rights*. Article 4th. VIRGINIA

 " ſhall

" ſhall be free from all taxes, cuſtoms, and " impoſitions, whatſoever, and none ſhall " be impoſed on them WITHOUT " CONSENT OF THE GENERAL " ASSEMBLY." An Appeal, (55) *&c.* p. 29.

I have dwelt much longer upon theſe *three Precedents* (cited by the Honourable Mr. Barrington) *againſt Ireland*, than I at firſt intended; but the ſeveral different ſubjects, to which I was naturally led

(55) This little tract contains a great deal of intelligence and ſound reaſoning concerning the natural Rights of mankind, and is highly worthy the peruſal of every good citizen who deſires information concerning the preſent differences with the Britiſh Colonies: and, upon the ſame occaſion, the clear and unanſwerable arguments of another able writer alſo, who ſigns himſelf "*Free Swiſs*," muſt not be forgot: The *title* of the work, laſt mentioned, ſeems indeed to be the *only* exceptionable part of it; *viz.* "*Great-Britain's Right* "*to tax her Colonies, placed in the cleareſt light, by a* "*Swiſs*;" for a *Right*, without a juſt foundation, cannot with *propriety* be intituled "*a Right*;" nevertheleſs he has, moſt certainly, "placed in *the cleareſt* "*light*" the *impropriety* of any ſuch claim upon the Colonies.

led in the examination of them, are of ſo much conſtitutional importance, and ſo neceſſary to be known to every Engliſhman, that I hope I may be excuſed for having, as they occurred, enlarged upon them, in the ſeveral Notes which I have added to my Text.

And, with reſpect to the *three Precedents* themſelves, I flatter myſelf that every impartial Reader, who carefully conſiders what has been already ſaid upon them, will freely pronounce them *illegal*, and totally unworthy of being allowed the leaſt weight or conſideration, as *Precedents*, againſt the *Independence* of *Ireland*, ſince they are equally capable of being retorted *as Precedents* for enſlaving even *England itſelf*: but I muſt therefore repeat what I have before declared, in p. 141 and elſewhere, that I am very ſure the worthy Writer, who unguardedly cited them, will be as zealous to

oppoſe

oppose any such doctrine as myself; and I believe that I may farther assure myself, that this learned Author will not be displeased or offended with the freedom of these remarks upon his Work; for, though I have not the honour to be personally acquainted with him, yet I am sufficiently acquainted (by other parts of his Writings) with the general benevolence and rectitude of his intentions, and also that he is an admirer and fast friend to our *constitutional Liberty* (which plainly appears in many other parts of his useful Work) as well as myself; so that any corrections, *on that side of the question*, will be taken (I dare say) by him as they were meant by me, that is, in good part, and without the least ill will: and his Work (I speak of it in general) has very deservedly acquired so much esteem and credit in the world, that I could not, without great injustice to the subject before me, permit any arguments therein,

upon

upon the point in queſtion, to remain unanſwered.

The ſame obſervation, I am inclined to think, is equally applicable, as well to the candour and diſpoſition, as to the writings, of Sir William Blackſtone, whoſe very learned and uſeful Commentaries muſt alſo be ſtrictly examined, upon this point, before I conclude my Declaration: and, had the other great and eminent writers (Lord Coke, Lord Chief Juſtice Vaughan, Judge Jenkins, *&c.*) whoſe opinions, upon the preſent ſubject, I am obliged alſo to call in queſtion, been ſtill alive, I ſhould have thought myſelf equally ſure of their benevolence and forgiveneſs, if I except Serjeant Mayart; becauſe the undeſerved contempt, with which he has treated Sir Richard Bolton, (the learned Author whom he attempted to anſwer,) prevents

my

my entertaining ſo charitable and friendly an opinion of him as I do of the reſt.

Though I have now drawn theſe remarks concerning the Conſtitution of *Ireland* to a much greater length than I at firſt propoſed, yet I muſt not conclude whilſt any material aſſertions of great authority remain unanſwered. Several of Sir Edward Coke's objections, on this head, have already, towards the beginning of this 2d part, been proved (I hope) to want *foundation:* but there ſtill remains to be conſidered a further doctrine, on the ſame point, advanced by him in *Calvin's Caſe*, which, I truſt, will appear to be *equally unjuſt*, though *founded* on the opinion of "*all the Judges* "*in England!*"

"In Anno 33 Reg. El." (ſays he) "it "was reſolved, by *all the Judges in En-* "*gland*, in the caſe of Orurke, *an Iriſh-* "*man*,

" *man*, who had committed High-" Treaſon *in Ireland*, that he, by the" Stat. of 33 Hen. VIII. c. 23. might" be indicted, arraigned, and tried, for" the ſame, *in England*, according to the" purview of the Statute." 7 Co. 448.

But this doctrine, notwithſtanding the great authority with which it is here delivered, is obnoxious to a *fundamental Right of the Subject*, the "*Trial by a Jury of* " *the* VICINAGE," or of "*Neighbours* " *to the Fact*," which is due to every private perſon in the Britiſh Dominions, according to the ancient Laws and Cuſtoms of this realm; otherwiſe the government would ceaſe to be *limited*, and thereby would ceaſe to be *lawful!* So that if Sir Edward Coke had been as much upon his guard, when he quoted this "*Reſolution of all the Judges*," as he was when he made his Remarks on that wicked Act of Parliament, in the reign of K. Hen. VII. by which alſo the *fundamental Right of Trial by Juries* was violated, he would neither have mentioned that Reſolution of "all the Judges," or even the Act itſelf, without guarding againſt the pernicious effects of ſuch an unconſtitutional doctrine, by a proper cenſure, as he did in the former caſe.

"It is not almoſt credible to foreſee" (ſays he) "when any *maxim* or *funda-* "*mental Law* of this realm *is altered,* "(as elſewhere hath been obſerved,) "what *dangerous inconveniences* do fol- "low; which moſt expreſsly appeareth "by this *moſt unjuſt and ſtrange* Act of "11 Hen. VII. for hereby not only "*Empſon* and *Dudley* themſelves, but "ſuch juſtices of peace," (corrupt men,) "as they cauſed to be authorized, com- "mitted moſt *grievous* and *heavy oppreſ-* "*ſions* and *exactions,* grinding of the face "of the poor ſubjects by penal laws;" "(be

" (be they never so obsolete or unfit for the " time,) by *information only*, without any " presentment or *Trial by Jury*, being " the antient *Birthright of the Subject*; " but to hear and determine the same " *by their discretion*, inflicting such pe- " nalty as *the Statutes not repealed imposed*, &c. 4th Inst. c. 1. p. 41.

And afterwards he adds: " This " Statute of 11 H. VII. we have recited, " and shewed *the just inconvenience there-* " *of*, to the end, *that the like* should never " hereafter be attempted *in any Court of* " *Parliament*. And that others might " avoid THE FEARFUL END OF " THESE TWO TIME-SERVERS, " *Empson* and *Dudley*. Qui eorum ves- " tigia insistunt, eorum exitus perhorres- " cant." (ibid.)

But, though these two wretched Judges were *hanged* for their *time-serving*, yet

 it

it appears, by this account of Lord Coke; that, when they presumed to dispense with the interposition of *Juries*, they acted by the *express Authority* of a *Statute*, or *Act of Parliament*; and, though they were *Time-servers*, so far as to acquiesce (contrary *to their Duty*, *as Judges*) in enforcing that wicked and unconstitutional Statute, (which exceeded the due bounds to which the English Legislature is necessarily *limited*,) yet, it seems, they *adjudged no penalties*, in consequence thereof, but such as "*the Statutes, not* "*repealed, imposed.*" And it is plain, therefore, that the crime of those two Judges (against which Lord Coke mentioned "the FEARFUL END *of those* "*two time-servers*," *as a warning to all future* JUDGES) consisted in allowing *the force of Law* to a wicked unconstitutional *Act of Parliament*, by which "*a* "FUNDAMENTAL LAW *of this realm*" (was) "*altered*;" so that their *crime* was exactly

exactly parallel to the (equally *criminal)* resolution of "*all the Judges in England,*" in the case of *Orurke* the *Irishman*, beforementioned, (which was, in like manner, founded on an express Act of Parliament, *viz.* 33 Hen. VIII. c. 23.) and parallel also to the crime (for it must be so esteemed) of "*all the Judges of* "*England,*" when they "resolved," in *Sir John Perrot's Case*, that, "*for a Treason* "*done in* IRELAND, *the offender may be tried,* "*by the Statute* 35 Hen. VIII. IN ENG-"LAND, because the words of the Statute "be, *All Treasons, committed out of the* "*Realm of England,* — and IRELAND is "out of the Realm of *England,*" &c. 3d Inst. p. 11. But the Judges, in both these cases, were quite as *inexcusable* as the two *time-servers,* Dudley and Empson; for, if the real *Intention* of the Legislature, by the said Acts of 33 and 35 Hen. VIII. had been so general as to include all places whatever, "out of the REALM *of Eng-*"*land,*"

" *land*," without leaving room for pleading a *legal* exception, in behalf of those territories wherein the laws, liberties, and constitution, of the Realm of England were already established, the said Judges ought to have known that " *a fundamental Law of this Realm*" was thereby " *altered*," and consequently that they incurred the risk of being HANGED, by some future administration, (like their *time-serving* predecessors,) for *presuming* to enforce such *unconstitutional Acts of Parliament*, by which, (according to the *just* Remark of the *same* great Reporter on a former Act, *viz.* 11 H. 7.) " *a fundamental Law of the Realm* (was) *altered*;" whereas, they really might have attributed a constitutional meaning to the said Acts, by duly distinguishing those (56) particular

(56) They might have alledged, that if an ambassador, sent from this kingdom to France, Spain, or to any other foreign State, *out of the Dominions* of the imperial Crown of Great-Britain, should notoriously betray his King and Country, and plot their Destruction, he

lar cases wherein they may LEGALLY be enforced, without thwarting any "fundamental Law of the Realm."

From

he might *legally* and *constitutionally* be punished according to the *letter* and *meaning* of the said Acts of Parliament; and also that any other British Subject whatsoever, that is, in like manner, *guilty of Treason* to his King and Country, during his residence in a foreign realm, may be treated accordingly; because all men certainly are accountable to their country for any such Treason; and, as they cannot be tried in the foreign realms, where the offences were committed, it is reasonable and just to suppose, that they may be tried in *England*, by an impartial Jury, though the same are not "*neighbours to the fact*," nor impannelled *de vicineto*, that is, from the neighbourhood where the offence was committed; for, though this circumstance is *essentially necessary to the Legality of a Jury* in every other case, yet the law does not require *impossibilities*, and it may therefore (perhaps) be *legally dispensed with*, when it is apparent, from the nature of the case, that such an unexceptionable Jury cannot be obtained, and yet that an exemplary punishment is manifestly due to the Traitor or Traitors: but when *Treasons* and other offences are committed in any country *under the dominion* of the Crown of *England*, where the criminals might have a *legal* Trial *according to the laws of this realm*, (as in *Ireland*,) the said *most essential formality* of being tried by a Jury *de vicineto* cannot be dispensed with; because this would deprive the Subject of an *unalienable Right*, and *alter* a "*fundamental Law of this* "*realm*;"

From what has been said, I hope it will appear sufficiently clear to my Readers,

ers,

" *realm* ;" so that any Judge, who should venture to enforce the said Acts, IN SUCH CASES, would manifestly DESERVE TO BE HANGED, as much as Dudley and Empson!

The examination of this point gives some general idea how far the *Power* of the high Court of Parliament (notwithstanding that imaginary " *omnipotency*" which some men have ignorantly attributed to it) may be allowed to extend; " for, the more high and absolute the jurisdiction of the court is, the MORE JUST and HONOURABLE it ought to be in the proceeding, and to give " example of Justice to inferior courts." 4th Inst. p. 37. Which is most strictly true; for, whenever the supreme temporal powers exceed the *honourable* limits of *natural Justice* and *Truth*, they lessen their own dignity, and, in proportion to their errors, forfeit that respectful consideration and esteem, which would otherwise be due from their subjects. And we must remember, likewise, that the being "*just and honourable*" in mere profession of words, without the *reality*, will have very little weight with the body of the *People*, who are endued with *common-sense*, as well as their superiors, to discern what is *just* and *honourable* from that which is *merely called so*; and that a pretence to *justice and honour*, in a bad cause, is only an aggravation of *injury* and *iniquity!* The most wicked ordinances have sometimes been ushered into the world under the most sanctified titles and specious pretences! The abominable Act beforementioned,

ers, that the severe censure, which Lord Coke so justly bestowed on the two wick-

 ed

tioned, of Hen. VII. was expresly said to be against "great enormities and offences, which" (have) "been "committed, and have daily, contrary to the *good* "*Statutes*, for many and divers behoovefull considera-"tions, severally made and ordained, to the displea-"sure of *Almighty God*, and the great let of *the com-"mon Law* and wealth of the land."

Now, notwithstanding this "FAIR FLATTERING "PREAMBLE," as Sir Edward Coke calls it, yet "THE PURVIEW *of that Act*" (as he justly remarked) "*tended, in the execution, contrary* EX DIAMETRO, viz. "*to the high displeasure of* ALMIGHTY GOD, *the great* "LET, *nay, the* UTTER SUBVERSION, *of the* COMMON "LAW, *and the* GREAT LET *of the Wealth of this Land*;" Ibid. p. 40. as, indeed, every other Act of Parliament must inevitably do, which perverts "*the due course of* "*the Law*," and robs the subjects of any *fundamental Right*.* And therefore, if any such Act should be made

* As for instance, let us suppose, (1st,) that an Act is made, to stop up or proscribe the passage to any *sea-port town*, or any *haven*, *shore of the sea*, or *great river*, without the Consent, and to the great Detriment, of all the neighbouring inhabitants; such an Act would be "FUNDAMENTALLY WRONG," as being contrary to the first or most essential Right of mankind, the *Law of Nature*: for it is clearly laid down by Bracton, that all *ports*, *havens*, *shores of the sea*, and *great rivers*, are free to all peaceable passengers, (but more particularly, we may add, to the nearest inhabitants,) by the *Law of Nature and of Nations*: "NATURALI VERO JURE *communia sunt* "*omnia hæc*, *aqua profluens*, *aer*, *et* MARE, *et* LITTORA MARIS, "quasi maris accessoria. NEMO enim ad littus maris accedere *pro-*"*hibetur*,

ed Judges, Dudley and Empson, for ACTING BY THE AUTHORITY OF

made in our days, (howsoever specious the preamble,) it is our duty, as good subjects, to rememb:r that the same

" *bibetur*, dum tamen a villis et ædificiis abstineat, quia littora sunt " DE JURE GENTIUM COMMUNIA, sicut et mare," *&c.* And again: " *Publica vero sunt* OMNIA FLUMINA *et* PORTUS, &c. " RIPARUM *etiam usus publicus est* DE JURE GENTIUM, *sicut ipsius* " *fluminis. Itaque naves ad eas applicare, funes arboribus ibi natis re-* " *ligare*, ONUS ALIQUÆ in eis reponere CUIVIS LIBER EST, sicuti " per ipsum fluvium navigare; sed proprietas earum est illorum quorum " prædiis adhærent," *&c.* lib. 1, c. 12, p. 7 & 8. So that such an Act would be manifestly contrary to the *Law of Nature* and *Nations*, and consequently is such as NO LEGISLATURE ON EARTH can render valid or *legal*, because *natural Rights* and the *Laws of Nature* are immutable, " *Jura enim naturalia sunt* IMMUTABILIA:" And again, " *Jura enim naturalia dicuntur* IMMUTABILIA, quia non possunt ex " toto ABROGARI VEL AUFERRI," *&c.* Ib. c. 5, p. 4. And besides, it must be remembered, that to proscribe the passage or *highway* to any city or town (especially if it is done with an avowed design to distress the inhabitants thereof in their lawful occupations) is an *intolerable nuisance*, which is clearly adjudged, in Law, to be such a " MALUM IN SE" as can *never be made lawful!* — " *But* MALUM " IN SE *the King* NOR ANY OTHER *can dispense*;" *Mes* MALUM " IN SE LE ROY NE NUL AUTRE poit dispenser, sicome le Roi " veut pardonner a occire un autre, ou lui licence A FAIRE NUSANCE " IN LE HAUT CHEMIN, CEO EST VOID," *&c.* 11 Hen. VII. p. 12. " Wherefore *it is generally true*" (as Judge Vaughan remarks) " *that* " MALUM PER SE *cannot be dispensed with*," *&c.* Rep. p. 334.

Or, 2dly, suppose an Act should be made, to impower the Governor of a Province, " *without the consent of the Council*," to appoint Judges and other Law-Officers, " *who shall hold their Commissions* " DURING THE PLEASURE OF" *the Crown*, instead of the approved and established *legal* condition, " *quamdiu se bene gesserint*;" thereby setting up WILL AND PLEASURE ABOVE LAW AND JUSTICE,

OF AN UNCONSTITUTIONAL ACT OF PARLIAMENT, is equally

 applicable

same ought to be considered as *null and void of itself*; and that it cannot authorize or indemnify the Judges, or

JUSTICE, which are the first and most essential Rights of the People! — Would not such an Act tend to "*the great* LET, nay the "UTTER SUBVERSION *of the Common-Law*," &c.? Suppose likewise it should be ordained, in such an Act, that "*the Freeholders* "*and Inhabitants of the several Townships*," in any particular province, shall *not* be permitted (even when "*they are authorized to* "*assemble together*) *to treat upon matters of the* MOST GENERAL CON-"CERN", — "*except the business* (be) *expressed in the leave given by* "*the Governor*;" which implies that *one* or a few individuals have a more *equitable* pretension "*to treat upon matters of the most* GENE-"RAL CONCERN" than even the *general Meeting*, or whole collective Body of persons themselves who are *concerned*! — a principle which is subversive of all "*common Right and natural Equity*;" and consequently must tend "to the high Displeasure of almighty God," as well as "*the great* LET *of the wealth of the land*." And, to compleat the iniquity of such an imaginary Act, let us suppose a clause, whereby "*it shall and may* BE LAWF L" (LAWFUL!) "*for the Justices*, &c. *in any Cause or Action which shall be brought to* "*issue, to order the said Cause or Action to be tried in* ANY COUNTY, "OTHER THAN THE COUNTY IN WHICH THE SAID CAUSE "OR ACTION SHALL HAVE BEEN BROUGHT OR LAID, BY A "JURY OF SUCH OTHER COUNTY, AS THEY SHALL JUDGE "FIT," *&c.* — Such a clause must strike at the very Foundation of Justice!

Or, 3dly, if this imaginary Act should not be esteemed sufficiently injurious to the People, (though it is apparently calculated to *rob them* of that *fundamental* and unalienable Right, "*the Trial by a Jury* "DE VICINETO,") let us suppose an Act still more PARTIAL (if possible) in the "*administration of Justice*!" and rendered still more aggravating and insulting by bearing a title "*contrary* EX DIA-"METRO" to the purport of it! — Let us (I say) endeavour to

stretch

applicable (for the very ſame reaſon) to the Reſolutions beforementioned, of "ALL

" THE

or any other perſons, who preſume to enforce it; for all men (and *Judges* in particular) ought to take warning,

ſtretch that notorious *Injuſtice* to the utmoſt extent of inconvenience and injury that a wicked imagination can poſſibly conceive or expreſs! that is, to eſtabliſh a Power of removing the Cauſes and Trials (and even thoſe which are of the moſt importance, *viz.* for *capital offences)* not only to a neighbouring *County*, or to a more diſtant *Colony*, but even, if caprice ſhould require it, to the furthermoſt extent of the Globe, that is, (without aggravation,) as far as *the Eaſt is from the Weſt!*

Or, 4thly, if we may conceive the idea of an Act calculated to " *fulfil the Meaſure of Iniquity,*" let us ſuppoſe an Act expreſsly for the purpoſe of eſtabliſhing the arbitrary Laws of France, (" *Quod* " *Principi placuit habet vigorem Legis,*" &c. ſee my Preface thereupon,) and, in order that it may be deſtructive to *the Souls*, as well as the *Bodies* and Property, of the wretched Subjects, (as I have already ſhewn,) let us ſuppoſe that ample proviſion is made therein for the *Eſtabliſhment* (not the mere Toleration) of downright *Idolatry* and *Image-Worſhip!* for the Toleration of the moſt notorious EXORCISMS (" *Exorciſmus Aquæ*;" — " *Exorciſmum Salis.*" — " *Ex-* " *orciſo te, creatura Salis*;" — ſee the Miſſal) and SPIRITUAL WITCHCRAFT! In ſhort, let us ſuppoſe that ſuch an Act provides for the Eſtabliſhment of that adulterated Religion which has long been perplexed with all the Enthuſiaſm of *heathen* ignorance, (*long Prayers, vain Repetitions,* " *as the Heathen do,*") and bears the moſt apparent marks of *Antichriſt*, inſomuch that we might be certain, at leaſt, who was the firſt *ſpiritual* Inſtigator and Promoter of ſuch a Bill, though the *bodily* Propoſer of it ſhould be lucky enough to remain undiſcovered! Who ſhall preſume to ſay, *that any Power on Earth* (whatſoever weak and ignorant men may think of the *Omnipotence* of Parliament) has Authority or Right, either to eſtabliſh ſuch notorious ſpiritual Abominations, or to render *lawful* ſuch groſs Iniquity and palpable Injuſtice!

" THE JUDGES IN ENGLAND," though Lord Coke himself (*even the author of the former*

ing, (from " *the fearful end* of those two time-servers, " Dudley and Empson,"), that such an active obedience would, perhaps, *endanger their own necks!* For suppose, 2dly, that such an Act was to be decked with the most flattering title; let us call it, for instance, " *An* " *Act for the* BETTER REGULATING *the government*" of any particular province; or, 3dly, let it be called " *An Act for* THE MORE IMPARTIAL ADMINIS-" TRATION OF JUSTICE, *in the cases of Persons* " *questioned for any acts done by them* IN THE EXECU-" TION OF THE LAW, *or for the Suppressi n* † *of Riots and* " *Tumults,*" &c. or, 4thly, suppose such an injurious and unlawful Act should be intitled " *An Act for making* " MORE EFFECTUAL PROVISION FOR THE GOVERN-" MENT OF" any particular province, *&c.* yet, if " *the Purview*" (as Lord Coke justly remarked) of any such imaginary Acts should " *tend, in the execution, con-*" *trary* EX DIAMETRO" to all these specious pretences, set forth in their titles and preambles, by establishing principles

† Though " *the Suppression of Riots and Tumults*" is here included as one of " *the fair flattering*" PRETENCES in the Title of the above-mentioned imaginary Act of Parliament, yet it it is apparent that the *wicked Act itself* would be the most effectual method that could possibly have been devised for THE PROMOTION, instead of " THE SUPPRESSION, *of Riots and Tumults*;" for which, consequently, none but the Promoters and Makers of such an unjust Law could, with any propriety, be esteemed accountable! since it is true, even to a maxim, that " He makes THE STRIFE (or "TUMULT") " *who first offends*" — " *Qui primum peccat, ille facit rixam.*" Prin. Leg. et Æquit. p. 92.

former censure) has cited them without the least animadversion!

The

principles whereby "*any fundamental Law* of the Realm "is altered," the same would manifestly *endanger the necks* (I must repeat it) of any Judges that were imprudent enough to enforce them, notwithstanding that the express Authority of *King*, *Lords*, and *Commons*, should be alledged as their sufficient warrant; because we find that the *like Authority* afforded no justification or excuse for poor Empson and Dudley, *in a similar case*, neither did the consideration of their having acted by *parliamentary Authority* render their wretched fate more pitiable in the eyes of the public! And therefore I sincerely wish that all modern *Time-servers* may have prudence enough to form (by that plain example) some reasonable judgement concerning the imaginary "*Omnipotence of Parliament*," which cannot insure its wretched votaries from the most ignominious punishment! nor secure even *the Parliament itself* from the just and lasting Censures of the Sages of our Law, such as *Lord Coke*, for instance, who warned them in another place, also, expressly upon this point: — "*By* "*colour of which Act*," (says he, meaning the said unjust Act of 11 Hen. VII.) "*shaking this* FUNDA- "MENTAL LAW," (the Law of Juries,) "*it is* "*not credible what* HORRIBLE OPPRESSIONS *and* EX- "ACTIONS, *to the undoing of infinite numbers of people*, "*were committed by* Sir Rich. Empson, Knt. *and* Edm. "Dudley, *&c. and, upon this* UNJUST *and* INJU- "RIOUS ACT, *(as commonly in like cases it falleth* "*out,) a new Office was erected*," &c. And in the next paragraph he adds, — "*And the* FEARFULL

"ENDS

The Judges, in the 33d year of Queen Elizabeth, who gave their opinion in the case of *Orurk*, (57) *the Irishman*, are the more inexcusable, for their *Resolution* upon the Act of 33 Hen. VIII. c. 23. because they had an *excellent Example* set them, but a few years before that time, by two very learned and respectable brethren, the Judges *Wray* and *Dyer*, (together with the said Queen's Attorney-General,) concerning several *similar Acts of Parliament*; which Example is worthy the most serious attention of *all future Judges*, that they may ever be *careful* to restrain, by a *legal* construction, not only the said Acts of King Henry VIII. and King Edward

" ENDS OF THESE TWO OPPRESSORS" (says he) " *should deterre others from committing the like, and* " *should* ADMONISH PARLIAMENTS, *that, in-* " *stead of this ordinary and pretious Trial* PER LEGEM " TERRÆ, *they bring not in absolute and partial Trials* " *by Discretion*." 2d Inst. p. 51.

(57) Or " *Ornick*." See 3d Inst. p. 11, margin.

Edward VI. but all others, likewise, that may happen to be equally liable to alter the free Constitution of the realm, and rob the subjects of any essential "*fundamental Right*," that ought to be esteemed *unalienable*.

Judge Dyer himself has reported the circumstances of it. He informs us (58) that "Gerrarde, Chauncelor of *Ireland*, "moved this question to the Queen's "Counsel, *viz.* Whether an Earl or "Lord of *Ireland*, who commits Trea-"son

(58) "*Gerrarde*, Chauncelor de *Irelande*, move cest "question al Counsel la Roygne, s. si un Countee "ou Seignior de *Irelande*, que commit Treason *in* "*Irelande* per overt Rebellion, serra arraygne et mis a "son tryall *in Engleterre* pour le offense, per l'estatute "de 26 H. 8. cap. 13. — 32 Hen. 8. cap. 4. — "35 H. 8. — 2 ou 5 Ed. 6. 11. — Et fuit tenus per "*Wray*, *Dyer*, et *Gerrarde*, Atturney General, QUE "IL NE POIT, *car il ne poit aver son tryal ici* PER "SES PEERES, NE PER ASCUN JURY DE XII. *pur* "*ceò que il n'est subject d'Engleterre, mes de Irelande, et* "*ideo* LA SERRA SON TRYAL. Et dictum est, "*que le usage la, d'attainder un Peere, est per Parlia-*"*ment, et nemy* per Pares." Dyer's Reports, p. 360 b.

" ſon by open Rebellion, ſhall be ar-
" raigned and put to his Trial *in Eng-*
" *land*, for the offence, by the Statute
" 26 H. VIII. c. 13. — 32 H. VIII.
" c. 4. — 35 H. VIII. — and 2 and 5
" Ed. VI. c. 11. And it was maintain-
" ed, by *Wray*, *Dyer*, and *Gerrarde*,
" the Attorney-General, that HE
" COULD NOT; *for he cannot have*
" *his Trial here* BY HIS PEERS, NOR BY
" ANY JURY OF 12, *becauſe that he is*
" *not a Subject of England*, but of *Ire-*
" *land*, and therefore his Trial ſhall be
" there," *&c.*

Theſe worthy Lawyers were not afraid, it ſeems, to maintain the weight of a LEGAL and FUNDAMENTAL REASON againſt the combined force of FOUR EXPRESS ACTS OF PARLIAMENT! And ſuch a reaſon, though it had been advanced only by *a ſingle Judge*, or even by *a private perſon*, is

 certainly

certainly of much more weight than the opinion of "*all the Judges in England*," when given *contrary to reason*, or against the tenor of *any fundamental Law*.

I never heard that *this Reason*, assigned by the Judges Wray and Dyer and the Attorney-General, against the force of the said *four Acts of Parliament*, has ever been questioned or disallowed as insufficient in the case of an *Irish Peer*; and therefore a similar reason is certainly as effectual in the case of any *private Irish Subject*, whose crime is *parallel*; because *true Justice* is *equal* in all her ways, and *has no respect to persons*. (59) For the same Law, which entitles the Nobleman to a Trial *by his Peers*, (60) secures also, to every

(59) "But if ye have *respect to persons*, YE COMMIT "SIN, *and are convinced of the Law* AS TRANSGRES-"SORS." James ii. 9.

(60) "*Per pares suos*," (Magna Charta, c. 14.) or "*per legale judicium* PARIUM SUORUM." Ib. c. 29.

every other perſon, his *parallel* Right to *a legal impartial Trial, by a Jury of honeſt unexceptionable* NEIGHBOURS: (61) for a Trial can neither be eſteemed *legal* or *impartial,* if the Jury are not impannelled in THE NEIGHBOURHOOD where the offence was committed; (62) unleſs we may except the ſingle caſe beforementioned, concerning treaſonable practices againſt *this Kingdom,* carried on by a Britiſh Subject in the dominion of a *foreign prince,* where the Crown of England *hath no juriſdiction:* but, in all other caſes whatſoever, the Trial by a Jury of *Neighbours to the Fact* is the unalienable RIGHT of all Britiſh Subjects, according to the

 ancient

(61) — "Per ſacramentum proborum et legalium "hominum DE VICINETO." Mag. Charta, c. 14.

(62) —— "Juſticiarii per Breve Regis ſcribunt "vicecomiti *comitatus* IN QUO FACTUM ILLUD "FIERI SUPPONITUR, quod ipſe venire faciat co-"ram eiſdem juſticiariis, ad certum diem per eos li-"mitatum, *duodecim probos et legales homines* DE VI-"CINETO *ubi illud factum ſupponitur;* qui neutram "partium ſic placitantium ulla affinitate attingunt." Forteſcue de Laud. Leg. Ang. c. 25. p. 54. b.

ancient LAW OF THE LAND: nay, this particular mode of Trial is so inseparably annexed to the *Law of the Land*, that it is sometimes expressed and known by that *general* term, "*the Law of the Land,*" (*Lex Terræ,*) as if there was no other *Law of the Land* but *this one*: which emphatical expression sufficiently proves that *this particular Law* for the Mode of Trials is the *first* and *most essential Law of the Constitution*; for, otherwise, it could not be entitled to such an eminent and peculiar distinction, in preference to all the other excellent *Laws of the Land*; and consequently this *principal or fundamental Law* is so necessarily *implied* and *comprehended*, in that general term, "*the Law of the Land*," that the latter may be considered as entirely *subverted* and *overthrown*, whenever the former is *changed* or *set aside*; for "*sublato fundamento* cadit opus." Jenk. Cent. 106.

In

In the 29th Chapter of Magna Charta, "*the Law of the Land*" seems to be mentioned in this peculiar sense: "*Nec super eum ibimus, nec super eum mittemus, nisi per legale judicium parium suorum, vel* PER LEGEM TERRÆ." Lord Coke refers us, "*for the true sense and exposition of these words,*" to "the Statute of 37 Ed. III. cap. 8." (meaning chapter the 18th,) "where the words, *by the Law of the Land,*" (says he,) "are rendered, *without due process of law,*" &c. which he farther explains, towards the end of the same sentence. — "That is," (says he,) "by *indictment or presentment of good and lawful men,* WHERE SUCH DEEDS BE DONE, *in due manner, or by Writ-Original of the Common-Law.*"

These last are the express words of another Act of Edw. III. (*viz.* 25 E. III. c. 4.)

c. 4.) (63) wherein they are given as an explanation of the words, "*by the Law* "*of the Land*," mentioned in the Great Charter. And the Great Charter itſelf, as well as this particular Act, and many other excellent Acts of K. Ed. III. is expreſsly cited and confirmed in an Act of the 16th Cha. I. c. 10. whereby the "*due Proceſs of the Law*" (or "*the or-*"*dinary Courſe of the Law*," ſee §. v.) is again re-eſtabliſhed, in oppoſition to the unlawful

(63) "Item, Whereas it is contained in the Great "Charter of the Franchiſes of *England*, that none "ſhall be impriſoned, nor put out of his Freehold, "nor of his Franchiſes nor free Cuſtom, unleſs it be "BY THE LAW OF THE LAND: It is accorded, "aſſented, and ſtabliſhed, that from henceforth none "ſhall be taken, by petition or ſuggeſtion made to "our Lord the King, or to his Council, unleſs it be "by *Indictment or Preſentment of his good and lawful* "*People* OF THE SAME NEIGHBOURHOOD WHERE "SUCH DEEDS BE DONE, in due manner, or by *Pro-*"*ceſs* made by writ-original at the Common Law. "Nor that none be put out of his Franchiſes, &c. un-"leſs he be DULY brought in anſwer, and fore-"judged of the ſame BY THE COURSE OF THE "LAW. And if any be done againſt the ſame, it "ſhall be redreſſed and HOLDEN FOR NONE." 25 Ed. III. c. 4.

unlawful authority that had been ufurped by the King, Privy-Council, and Star-Chamber.

This "*due Procefs of the Law,*" therefore, can be no otherwife than by a legal Jury of 12 credible men, (64) *who are Neighbours to the Fact*, and *unexceptionable* to the parties concerned, according to the *ancient Cuftom* or *Law of the Land.* (65) And that the fame is alfo a *fundamental* and *effential* Right of the Subject, every man, who pretends to doubt of it, may be

(64) —— "In prefentia *duodecim* fide dignorum "virorum FACTO VICINORUM, de quo agitur, "et circumftantiis ejus: qui et nofcunt eorundem "teftium mores, maxime fi VICINI ipfi fuerint nof- "cunt etiam, et fi ipfi fint credulitate digni," *&c.* Fortefcue de Laud. Leg. Ang. c. 28, p. 64. See alfo the 25 and 26th chapters of that excellent little book.

(65) "Item per *antiquam Legem,* et confuetudinem "*Regni,* omnes exitus quæ emergent *in aliqua Curia* "*de Recordo* infra Regnum, nifi pauci de quibus non "eft hic neceffe tractandum, debet triari per xii. li- "beros et legales homines DE VICINETO, *&c.* "qui nulli partium ulla affinitati attingent." Doct. & Stud. c. 7. p. 26 b.

be informed *by the feelings of his own breast*, if he will only take the trouble, for a moment, to suppose *himself* in such a situation, (through the false accusations of his enemies,) that nothing but an impartial Trial, by *a Jury of Neighbours*, well acquainted with him and his case, and the malignity of his accusers, can possibly save him from destruction! And farther, it is apparent, that the said "*due* "*Process of the Law*," by a Jury *de vicineto*, is now become an *unalterable* part of the Constitution, and must ever remain in force, not only against all contrary *Resolutions* and *Opinions of the Judges*, (such as I have mentioned,) but even against the express authority of any Act of Parliament that happens (inadvertently) to have been made to the contrary, because all such must necessarily "BE "HOLDEN FOR NONE," according to the 42. Ed. III. c. 1. which is cited by by Judge Jenkins for that purpose: (66) and, though it may be alledged, against the authority of this Act of Parliament, that another Act may unbind what it has bound, according to the maxim, "*eodem* "*modo quo quid constituitur, eodem modo* "*dissolvitur*:" yet a due consideration of *this very maxim* will afford us a substantial argument to the contrary: for, at the time the said Act was made, (*viz.* in the 42. Ed. III.) the *Great Charter* had been *expressly confirmed by many Parliaments*, not only in the reigns of that noble king's ancestors, but also by at least TWELVE *preceding Parliaments* (67) even in his own glorious reign; so that the Parliament, in his 42d year, had certainly suf-

 ficient

(66) Jenkinsius Redivivus, p. 65.

(67) And *Parliaments* at that time were preserved *in purity and independence by a very frequent renewal of* THE POPULAR REPRESENTATION, *viz.* "*every year once*, "*and* MORE OFTEN *if* (there was) *need*," &c. which I have already proved in pages 166 to 170 of this Declaration; so that there was not then the least room even for the bare *suspicion* of undue influence!

ficient authority to add, to their confirmation of the Charters, that, "*if* ANY "STATUTE *be made to the contrary, that* "*shall be* HOLDEN FOR NONE." And the reason is plain; for no Statute whatever *(eodem modo constituitur)* is ordained by so *great Authority* as that which *Magna Charta* has at length acquired, by the express confirmation, from time to time, of *so many different Kings and Parliaments:* (68) The wisdom of ages has made it venerable, and stamped it with an authority equal to the *Constitution* itself, of which it is, in reality, a most essential and *fundamental* part; so that any attempt to repeal (69) it would be treason

(68) In the time of Sir Edward Coke the Charters had been expresly confirmed by THIRTY-TWO DIFFERENT PARLIAMENTS, as he himself witnesses in the Proeme of his 2d Institute: "*The said* "2 *Charters*" (says he) "*have been confirmed, established, and commanded to be put in execution, by* 32 *several Acts of Parliament.*"

(69) Though some particular articles of Magna Charta are indeed rendered useless, at this day, by subsequent

treaſon to the ſtate! This glorious Charter muſt, therefore, ever continue unrepealed: and even the articles, which ſeem at preſent uſeleſs, muſt ever remain in force, to prevent the *Oppreſſions and Prerogatives*, there named, from being extended beyond *certain limits*, in caſe the ſame ſhould ever hereafter be revived. No ſingle Act of Parliament can unbind

ſubſequent Statutes, yet this affords no argument againſt the general ſtability of the Charter, with reſpect to its main object, the Freedom of the People. It is a Charter of Liberties, and therefore the ſubſequent Statutes, which *enlarged thoſe Liberties*, (by annihilating the ſeveral oppreſſive cuſtoms which are mentioned therein and limited within certain bounds, as *Knights Service*, *Eſcuage*, *Wards*, and *Liveries*, &c.) cannot be ſaid to *operate againſt* the Charter, but rather *in aid of it*; for though the ſaid oppreſſive Tenures and dangerous Prerogatives are permitted by the Charter in *a certain degree*, yet the apparent intention of the ſeveral articles, wherein they are mentioned, was not to *eſtabliſh*, but only to *reſtrain* them, as much as the circumſtances, temper, and prejudices of thoſe early times would permit: ſo that the Statutes, which afterwards entirely removed the oppreſſion, cannot be eſteemed contrary to the purpoſe of the Charter, becauſe they enlarged thoſe Liberties and Franchiſes of the people, to which the Charter itſelf is ſo apparently dedicated.

or remove the limits here laid down: nothing less than the same *accumulated Authority*, by which the Charter is now established, can possibly set it aside, or any part of it, according to *the Maxim* before recited, "*eodem modo quo quid constituitur, eodem modo dissolvitur*:" for no single Act of Parliament, "*eodem modo constituitur*," is ordained in the *same manner*. The many repeated confirmations of its authority were a work of ages; so that the said authority cannot *legally* be set aside, unless it be done *eodem modo quo constituitur*, that is, by the repeated suffrages of *as many Parliaments against it* as have already expressly confirmed it; and God forbid that any such gross depravity and corruption should ever obtain such a continuance in this kingdom, as to accomplish so great an evil; for that could not be without a total national reprobacy, dangerous to us not only in this world, but also in the next!

It

It muſt, therefore, be obvious to every perſon, who duly conſiders all theſe circumſtances, that *the Reſolutions of* "ALL "THE JUDGES IN ENGLAND," in the caſes of *Orurke*, or *Ornicke*, *the Iriſhman*, and *Sir John Perrot*, were contrary to a FUNDAMENTAL LAW in the *Great Charter*, and conſequently ought to be "HOLDEN FOR NONE," according to the expreſs determination of the Parliament, in the 42d Ed. III. c. 1. (70) and ought to be "VOID IN THE LAW "*and* HOLDEN FOR ERROUR," according to the ſecond chapter (71) of the ſame

(70) *Viz.* "That the *Great Charter*, and the *Charter of the Foreſt* be holden and kept in all points; "and if *any Statute be made to the contrary*, THAT "SHALL BE HOLDEN FOR NONE."

(71) —— "It is aſſented and accorded, for the "good governance of the *Commons*, that no man be "put to anſwer, without Preſentment before Juſtices, "or matter of Record, or by DUE PROCESS AND "WRIT ORIGINAL, *according to the* OLD LAW "OF THE LAND" (which I have already proved to

ſame excellent Statute; becauſe the two Acts of Parliament, of the 33 and 35 H. 8. on which they grounded their opinion, cannot have any *legal* force, (notwithſtanding the *literal* meaning of the *general expreſſions* therein,) when applied to offences committed in any country, province, or *colony* whatſoever, that is ſubject to the imperial crown of Great-Britain: ſo that even if *Ireland* had been "*eſpecially named*" therein, the ſaid Acts would have been ſo far from *binding* that kingdom, (according to the effect ſuppoſed by Lord Coke, Judge Vaughan, Judge Blackſtone, and others,) that the very NAMING *Ireland*, for ſuch purpoſes as were intended by the ſaid Acts, would have rendered them *abſolutely* "NULL AND VOID," and to be "HOLDEN FOR NONE," becauſe they would, in that caſe, have been directly

to ſignify, in an *eſpecial* manner, the Trial by a Jury of the *Vicinage)*; "*and if* ANY THING, *from henceforth, be done to the contrary, it ſhall be* VOID IN THE LAW *and holden for Error.*"

rectly *contrary* to the *Great Charter*; whereas, at present, there are ſome particular caſes (as I have before remarked) wherein they may, perhaps, be allowed a legal force.

Now, though what I have already remarked will probably be thought a *ſufficient* Anſwer to the two Reſolutions "*of* "*all the Judges in England*," cited by *Lord Coke* as precedents againſt the Liberties of our brethren, *the ſubjects of* IRELAND, I am nevertheleſs inclined to add one more eſtimony againſt the ſaid *Reſolutions*, which has no leſs authority than that even of *Lord Coke himſelf* (in another part of his writings) againſt all *ſimilar* Reſolutions and Opinions!

Let him now bear witneſs both againſt the ſaid *Judges* and *himſelf!* — "And "albeit, Judgements in the King's "Courts" (ſays he) "are of high regard "in "in Law, and *judicia* are accounted as "*juris-dicta*, yet it is provided, by Act "of Parliament, that if *any Judgement be* "*given contrary to any of the points of* "*the Great Charter or Charta de Foresta*, "BY THE JUSTICES, *or by any other of* "*the King's Ministers*, &c. *it shall be* "*undone and* HOLDEN FOR "NOUGHT." Proeme to his 2d Institute.

If Lord Coke, when he mentioned the BINDING IRELAND in the Parliament of *England*, "BY SPECIAL WORDS," (4th Inst. p. 350.) and "BY BEING ESPECIALLY "NAMED," (Calvin's Case, 7th Rep. p. 447.) had meant nothing more than what is clearly proved by his "*one exam-*"*ple for all*," beforementioned, (*viz.* that a Representation of the Subjects in *Ireland* ought to be summoned to the *English* Parliament, whenever "*an Act of* "*Parliament shall be made in England*" (especially)

(eſpecially) "*concerning the Statute of* "*Ireland,)*" there would have been no eſſential difference between *his Opinion* and that *natural Juſtice* for which I contend: but, alas! that great man has confirmed his error upon that ſubject in another part of *Calvin's Caſe*, (p. 446,) wherein he declares "*that albeit* IRE- "LAND *was a diſtinct dominion, yet,* "THE TITLE THEREOF BEING BY "CONQUEST, *the ſame by* judgement of "law *might by expreſs words be bound* "*by Act of the Parliament of England.*" Here he has luckily given us another *reaſon*, which leads us to the detection of his error. — "*Yet*" (ſays he) "THE "TITLE THEREOF BEING BY CON- "QUEST," *&c.* Now, it is very remarkable, that ſo many of the moſt eminent law writers ſhould have *copied* and *adopted* this erroneous opinion, without *examining the force of it*; as if the authority and real worth of this learned Writer,

 in

in other reſpects, were ſufficient to render valid a *miſtaken and groundleſs argument!* Judge Jenkins, indeed, has *adopted* the opinion without quoting *the reaſons*; but Judge Vaughan, who has alſo *adopted* the opinion, refers us expreſsly to Lord Coke's *reaſon* againſt *Ireland*, *viz.* "the "*title by conqueſt.*" — "That it is a CON-"QUERED KINGDOM" (ſays he) "*is not* "*doubted, but admitted* IN CALVIN'S "CASE, *ſeveral times*," &c. Vaughan's Rep. p. 292. And, upon the ſtrength of this *reaſon*, he proceeds very confidently to "determine *what things the Parliament of* "*Ireland cannot do*," and to give inſtances "*of Laws made in the Parliament of* "ENGLAND *binding* IRELAND;" p. 293. of which neither the firſt (72) nor the ſecond

(72) A Law concerning the Homage of Parceners, called, "*Statutum Hiberniæ*," 14 Hen. III. — "Mr. Cay" (ſays the Hon. Mr. Barrington) "very "properly obſerves, that 'IT IS NOT AN ACT OF "PARLIAMENT,' and cites the old Abridgement, "title *Homage*. He allows it a place, however, in "his

ſecond (73) are in the leaſt intitled to the name of "*Laws made in the Parliament*

"*of*

" his edition of the Statutes, not to differ from for- " mer editors. This, in ſome meaſure, gives the au- " thority of Legiſlation" (ſays this learned Gentleman, ironically) " to the King's Law-Printers: and " yet, if ſuch an ordinance is inſerted in every edition " of the Statutes, for near 3 centuries together, by " printers known to print under the authority of the " King's Patent, and the Parliament permits this for " ſuch a length of time, it becomes a queſtion of " ſome difficulty to ſay what force it may have ac- " quired. No ſuch queſtion fortunately can ever a- " riſe upon this Statute, *as it is merely a* RESCRIP- " TUM PRINCIPIS to certain *Milites* (Adventurers, " probably, in the Conqueſt of *Ireland*, or their De- " ſcendants) who had doubts with regard to the Te- " nure of lands holden by Knights Service and de- " ſcending to Co-parceners within age," *&c.* Obſervations on the more ancient Statutes, p. 39.

(73) A Statute of Nottingham, called " Ordina- " natio pro Statu Hiberniæ," 17 E. 1. — Upon which the Hon. Mr. Barrington remarks: " It is very " ſingular" (ſays he) " that, though this Ordinance " hath found a place amongſt the *Engliſh* Acts of Par- " liament, the Collection of *Iriſh* Statutes, printed by " authority at Dublin, begins only with the Ordi- " nances of *Kilkenny*, in the 3d year of Edward the " 2d. There can be no doubt, however, that this " Law extends to *Ireland*, if not repealed by ſome " *Iriſh* Act of Parliament; as, by Poyning's Law, in

" the

" *of England,*" though they are printed in the Statute-Books. (74)

Amongst

" the time of Henry the Seventh, *all precedent* Eng-" lish Statutes are made to bind in *Ireland.*" Ib. p. 141. Nevertheless I must beg leave to observe, that this is neither an *English* nor an *Irish* Statute, but a mere *Letter-Patent* of the King, *by the Assent of his Council* (though it might be dated, perhaps, during the sittings of a Parliament at Nottingham) : — " Edward, " par la grace de Dieu, Roy Dengliterre, Seignor " Dirland, &c. — a toutes ceux, que ceux Letters " verront ou oiront, salutes. Saches que a le men-" dement de gulement de nostre terre Dirlande, a " pluis grand peax et tranquill. de nostre people en cel " terre a Notin. as octaves del St. Martin, &c. par " *assent de nostre Counsell illonques,*" &c. This is not the stile of an Act of Parliament; neither is the Assent of the *common Council,* or *general Council* expressed, but only " *by the Assent of* OUR COUNCIL," that is, *the King's Council,* which is always understood to signify the Privy-Council, and not the *national Council.* Besides, the King expresly calls this Ordinance, " OUR " LETTERS-PATENT," and witnessed it as such, in the usual form, *viz.* " *En tesmoignance* de quel chose " nous avons fait faire CESTES NOUS LETTERS " OVERTES. *Done a Notyngham le* 24 *jour de No-" vembre, lan de nostre reigne dix septisme.*" Secunda Pars Veterum Statutorum, printed ann. 1555, p. 68 & 69.

(74) This seems also to be the case with the 3d voucher which he has produced for his assertion, *viz.* " *Laws for* IRELAND, made by E. 3, per advisa-" mentum.

Amongst the *modern* writers, who have likewise unfortunately *adopted* the same erroneous

" mentum Concilii nostri," &c. That is, if he meant the Laws contained in the Ordinance of that King's 31st year, *viz.* " Ordinatio facta pro Statu " Terræ Hiberniæ ;" because this Ordinance is no more intitled to the name of *a Law*, or *Act of Parliament*, than the two former ; for, long before this period, the necessity of expressing *the Assent of the Commons*, in order to render an Act *valid*, was well understood, as the Hon. Mr. Barrington remarks, on the 14th of Ed. III. " *The Statutes now begin to appear*" (says he) " *in a new, and more regular form* ; &c. *whilst the Pre-*" *amble*, IN EVERY INSTANCE, *makes express men-*" *tion of the* CONCURRENCE OF THE COMMONS," p. 218 ; whereas this Ordinance has no such mention of their " CONCURRENCE," but only the *Assent of the Council*, that is, the Assent of the *King*'s Council — " *de assensu consilii nostri ordinanda duximus*," &c. whereas the Assent of the *great Council of the Nation* is expressed in very different terms, as I have remarked in the former notes, as also in the notes on pages 128 and 129.

But if this learned Judge meant any other Laws " *for* IRELAND, *made by Edward* III." than this Ordinance of his 31st year, (for he refers us, in the margin, to the Parliament-Rolls of his 5th year,) yet the same cannot afford the least proof or precedent for *binding Ireland* in England without Assent, because I have already cited ample testimony that the Parliament of

erroneous opinion of Lord Coke, the learned Judge Blackstone is the most eminent,

of *Ireland* in those days was frequently summoned to *England*, sometimes to confer with the *English* Parliament, and sometimes to meet the King and his Council in distinct Sessions of the *Irish* Legislature. See pages 66 to 80.

His fourth voucher adds no more confirmation to his assertion than the three former; for though it is really *an Act of Parliament*, yet it cannot be produced as a precedent for *binding* the *Irish* Subjects *without their Consent*, because it is made expresly for the purpose of *enforcing* an Act of the *Irish Parliament*, "*Estatute fait en la terre d'Ireland*;" and therefore, as the question relates only to the carrying the said Law into execution, which is properly the office of the King and his Courts, it is certainly indifferent whether he is advised therein by his *Privy-Council* or by his *Common-Council* of *England*, especially as the latter, in the case before us, were so far from advising the King to invade or alter the *Irish* Law, that they confirm it in the strongest terms — "*que le dit Estatute estoise* EN SA ENTIER FORCE, *et que bien et duement soit gardez et* PLEINEMENT EXECUTE, *&c.*

With respect to his 5th voucher, referring us to "*the late Acts made in* 17 *Car.* 1," &c. it would be very unfair to draw from thence any conclusions unfavourable to the Privileges of the *Irish* Parliament, because that was the fatal year of the popish massacre in *Ireland*, when the Protestant Subjects of that kingdom were almost universally oppressed, and all Law and Regularity overturned by the open Rebellion of the popish

eminent, and therefore demands the most careful examination.

In

popish party: so that even the Parliament of *Scotland* (as well as the Parliament of *England)* thought it right to take the affairs of *Ireland* under their consideration at that unfortunate juncture; and sent two Commissioners, properly instructed by the States of that kingdom, to treat with the *English* Parliament about the means of suppressing the *Irish* Rebellion. Sir John Temple's History of the Irish Rebellion, p. 156 to 158.

But notwithstanding that some Acts might have been made in the 17th of Charles I. without the Assent of the *Irish* Parliament, yet they afford no evidence in favour of that opinion for which they are cited by the learned Judge; for Mr. Molyneux has proved that, by the repeal of those very Acts of 17 Cha. I. that they afford an argument even on the *other side of the question*, viz. "*that the Parliament of* "IRELAND *may repeal an Act made in* ENGLAND *in* "*relation to the affairs of* IRELAND," p. 75.

And again, with respect to the 6th and last voucher, under that head, (*viz.* the resolution of the Judges in the Exchequer-Chamber, in the case of the Merchants of Waterford,) it by no means relates to the question in dispute; for that concerns only the exportation and importation of goods, and the *Irish* do not pretend to contest the Right of Great-Britain to the *Dominion of the Seas*; nor do they deny the Power of the British Parliament to regulate Commerce, as I have before remarked. Now, as it appears that *not one* of these Precedents is sufficient for the purpose proposed,

In the introduction to his Commentaries, p. 101, he hath delivered his sentiments much to the same effect as the other more ancient writers, already mentioned. — That "*no Acts of the* ENGLISH "*Parliament, since the twelfth of King* "*John, extended into that kingdom,*" (Ireland,) "*unless it were* SPECIALLY "NAMED, *or* INCLUDED UNDER GENE-"RAL WORDS, *such as* WITHIN ANY "OF THE KING'S DOMINIONS," *&c.* And in page 103 he repeats the same doctrine, "that no Acts of the English "Parliament made since the 10th "Hen. VII. do now *bind* the people of "*Ireland*, unless SPECIALLY NAMED "or INCLUDED UNDER GENERAL "WORDS."

posed, and as we cannot doubt but that so learned a Lawyer as Judge Vaughan (as I have before observed of Judge Coke) would select the most applicable Precedents that could be found, the doctrine which he has built upon these insufficient Precedents must necessarily fall to the ground.

" WORDS." (75) And in the ſame paragraph he aſſigns the very ſame reaſon (drawn from *the Conqueſt* of *Ireland)* which had miſled both Lord Coke and Judge Vaughan before him. " *And, on* " *the other hand,*" (ſays he,) "*it is* EQUAL-" LY CLEAR, *that, where Ireland is par-*" *ticularly named, or* IS INCLUDED UN-" DER GENERAL WORDS, *they are* BOUND " *by ſuch Acts of Parliament.*" (though I hope I have already made *the contrary* appear EQUALLY CLEAR.) " *For this* " *follows*"

(75) For this *incluſive* Power, of GENERAL WORDS, Judge Blackſtone refers us to Lord Coke's 12. Rep. 112. but I ſhall take no pains to refute any error in that *laſt Collection* of his Reports, " *which are well known*" (ſays the honourable Mr. Barrington, p. 161) " *not to be of* " *equal authority with thoſe that precede.*" And beſides, I have already demonſtrated, (I hope,) in my Comment on the Caſes of *Orurke*, the *Iriſhman*, and *Sir John Perrot*, (as alſo by the clear and deciſive Reſolution of the worthy Judges, *Wray* and *Dyer*, and the Attorney-General *Gerrard*, for reſtraining the GENERAL WORDS of *four expreſs Acts of Parliament*,) that all ſuch *general Words*, in Statutes, muſt be duly reſtrained by a *legal Conſtruction*, if the Judges, who enforce them, mean to avoid the Riſk of exemplary puniſhment!

"*follows*" (ſays he) "*from the very na-*
"*ture and conſtitution of a* DEPENDENT
"STATE: *dependence being very little elſe*
"*but an* OBLIGATION TO CONFORM TO
"THE WILL OR LAW OF THAT
"SUPERIOR PERSON OR STATE (76)
"*upon*

(76) The *Iriſh* do not pretend to deny a *legal Dependence* on the ſuperior State of *England*, for they acknowledge that the Sovereignty of their Iſland is inſeparably annexed to the Crown of *England*, of which, I believe, I have already quoted ſome examples: but, when *Dependence* is defined (in the manner Judge Blackſtone repreſents it) as "*an Obligation to conform to the Will or* "*Law* of the ſuperior Perſon or State," &c. it ceaſes to be a *legal* Dependence, according to the *common Law and Conſtitution of England*; though the learned Judge is certainly right enough, if he will be pleaſed to confine his Definition of *Dependence* to thoſe Countries where the *civil Law* prevails, as in *France* or *Pruſſia* for inſtance; becauſe, in ſuch deſpotic Realms, the oppreſſed People ſeem, indeed, to acknowledge "an "Obligation to conform to the *Will* or *Law* of the *ſu-* "*perior Perſon or State*;" and the learned Commentator, if he meant to refer to the Laws of ſuch enſlaved People as theſe, muſt certainly be allowed to have delivered his meaning in the moſt *expreſſive* and *judicious* terms that he could poſſibly have choſen *for ſuch a purpoſe*; for, in ſpeaking of "*the Will*" of "*that ſuperior Perſon or* "*State*" to which he ſuppoſes "*an Obligation to con-* "*form*," &c. he mentions it as a ſynonimous term to the

" *upon which the inferior depends.*" And then he immediately adds: " *The original*

the word " *Law,*" *viz.* " *Will or Law,*" ſays he, that is, " an Obligation to conform to the *Will or Law* " of that ſuperior Perſon or State," *&c.* which is, indeed, a moſt lively deſcription of the dangerous *unlimited* Power of the French, Pruſſian, or Imperial, Adminiſtrations of Government; for, whereſoever theſe two words, WILL *and* LAW, are conſidered as ſynonimous, there *Law* muſt, of courſe, be any thing (be it ever ſo wicked or iniquitous) that the Superior pleaſes; that is, in ſhort, " *Quod Principi placuit Legis habet Vi-* " *gorem !*" But I have already held up that deteſtable Maxim of the *civil Law* to the view of my Readers; and therefore I ſhall now only remark, in general, that neither the LAWS of *England* nor the LAWS of *Ireland* acknowledge any ſuch Precept as the ſetting up the WILL of a Superior for LAW; or, (what is the ſame thing,) they do not acknowledge any ſuch ſtate of " *Dependence*" as an OBLIGATION *to conform to the* " WILL OR LAW" (thoſe ſynonimous Terms) " *of* " *the ſuperior Perſon or State,*" *&c.*

Our Laws, indeed, acknowledge the King of Great-Britain for the time being as the " *Superior*" or *Head* of both Kingdoms; but the " *Dependence,*" which is thereby required of " *the Inferior,*" (whether the term, *inferior*, be applied to the inferior Kingdom as *ſubordinate*, or to Perſons, *viz.* to each Individual as *a Subject,)* in either caſe, is a *politic* or *legal* " *Dependence,*" and not *abſolute* and *unlimited.* — " *Principatu namque* " *nedum* REGALI, *ſed et* POLITICO, *ipſe ſuo populo dominatur.*"

" *and true ground*" (says he) " *of this*
" *Superiority, in the present case, is what*
" *we*

" *natur.*" The Laws leave no room to suppose that there is " *an Obligation to conform to the* WILL *or* LAW" (if the latter has no other foundation than the *Will)* " *of* " *that superior Person.*" " *Nam non potest Rex Angliæ* AD " LIBITUM SUUM *Leges mutare Regni sui. Principatu* " *namque nedum* REGALI," &c. as above. (Fortescue de Laud. Leg. Angliæ, c. 9. p. 25 b.) And, if even the *King's* Power is not *regal*, but *politic* and *limited*, (which the same learned Writer, Chancellor Fortescue, has clearly proved in a distinct Tract, expresly on that subject, intitled, " The Difference between *absolute* " and *limited* Monarchy,") much less can the *King's Subjects* be said to exercise a " *Sovereign's legislative* " *Power*" (1. Com. p. 101) over any Nation or People whatsoever, that have no share in the said Power by a due *Representation* of their own collective body: for the *sovereign Majesty of the People* ought never to be exerted, except in their own necessary defence, or to maintain the *natural Rights* and *equitable Privileges* of Mankind, against Tyrants and Oppressors, for the good of Society in general, through that disinterested evangelical Principle, " *Good-will towards men.*" But when, on the contrary, any particular Nation or People exerts that " *sovereign legislative Power*" to deprive another different Nation of their *natural Rights and Liberties*, they no longer deserve to enjoy their *own*; and, indeed, *divine* JUSTICE will inevitably overtake them sooner or later; for, as the crimes of individuals will surely be punished with *personal* condemnation, so *national sins* must feel the additional Weight of temporal *national*

" *we uſually call, though ſomewhat* IM-" PROPERLY," (very " IMPROPERLY" indeed,) " THE RIGHT OF CONQUEST:" *&c.* Now, I moſt heartily join with him in his application of the adverb " IMPRO-" PERLY" to the words which follow, *viz.* " THE RIGHT OF CONQUEST," whenever it is mentioned as a *reaſon* to juſtify this claim or imaginary right of binding the people of *Ireland*, either by being " *ſpecially named* or included under " *general words*;" for I hope I ſhall convince that learned gentleman himſelf, as well as the reſt of my readers, before I conclude, that " THE RIGHT OF CON-" QUEST" is not " *the original and true* " *ground*" of any ſuch " *ſuperiority, in the* " *preſent caſe*," as he ſuppoſes; but, on the contrary, that it ſeems rather to have been

national Retribution; which, I truſt, I have demonſtrated in a little Tract, intended ſometime or other for Publication, intitled, " *The Law of Retribution, and,* " *in particular, of God's temporal Vengeance on Slave-* " *holders.*"

been "*the original and true ground*" of all the dangerous miſtakes which have been made, upon this important queſtion, by Lord Coke, Judge Vaughan, and himſelf: for, if this learned gentleman will be pleaſed to review this argument, founded on "*the Right of Conqueſt*," as applied by himſelf and the other two very eminent Writers, beforementioned, to the free kingdom of *Ireland*, I truſt (through the great opinion I entertain of his candour and good ſenſe) that he will readily give it up; for, though the "*Right of* "*Conqueſt*" may be, as he ſays, "*a Right* "*allowed by* THE LAW OF NATIONS, *if* "*not by that of Nature*," (that is, in ſome particular caſes,) yet it certainly is contrary both to "*the Law of Nations*" and "*that of Nature*," (to which he has appealed,) that "*the Right of Conqueſt*" ſhould be pleaded for *binding* the *Conquerors themſelves, or their Deſcendants, without their Aſſent!* for of ſuch conſiſt the greateſt

greateſt part of the landed intereſt in *Ireland*, at this day, who are entitled to all the Rights and Liberties of the ANCIENT CONQUERORS by *inheritance* and *lineal deſcent*: — Titles ſo *juſt* and *ſacred*, that I am ſure Judge Blackſtone will never perſiſt in oppoſing them; eſpecially when he ſees hereafter by what authority I make this aſſertion: Nay, the "*Right of Con-"queſt*" is ſo bad a plea to extenuate the *iniquity* of exerting any ſuch oppreſſive and *unlimited* power, that it fails in *Reaſon* and in natural *Juſtice*, even when applied as an excuſe for oppreſſing *the conquered*; — much leſs therefore can it affect the Liberties and natural Rights of the *Conquerors* themſelves!

That theſe *Liberties* and *natural Rights* of the *conquerors* are entailed upon a very great part (if not the moſt *numerous*, at leaſt the moſt *conſiderable in point of rank and fortune*) of the preſent inhabitants

tants of *Ireland*, is a point, I believe, which cannot be contested; for Judge Blackstone himself has declared in a preceding page, 99: ——" *That the in-* " *habitants of* IRELAND are, FOR THE " MOST PART (77), *descended from the* " ENGLISH, who planted it *as a kind of* " COLONY, *after the Conquest* of it by " King Henry the Second," *&c.* and consequently " THE MOST PART" of the said Inhabitants ought to be considered as standing in the place of the *Conquerors*, rather than of the *Conquered*, so that if the *Reason* assigned by these three learned men has *any weight*, *viz.* that some degree of *superiority* is acquired by *Right of Conquest*, it must be allowed, that " THE " MOST

(77) The following Extract, from Sir Wm. Petty's Political Survey of Ireland, will corroborate this just Remark of Sir William Blackstone.——" The *British* " Protestants and Church have three-fourths of all the " Lands, five-sixths of all the housing, nine-tenths of " all the housing in walled towns and places of " strength, two-thirds of the foreign trade," *&c.* p. 27.

MOST PART of the ſaid Inhabitants are equally intitled to it, in Right of their *conquering Anceſtors*; for it would be highly injurious to deprive them of their *hereditary Privileges*, which deſcend to them from the actual Conquerors themſelves.——And, on the other hand, it would be equally *unjuſt*, *wicked*, and *impolitic*, to make any partial diſtinction between them and the deſcendants of the *conquered Iriſh*, who, after many years ſtruggle, are now, at laſt, happily incorporated and blended with them as *one free People!*

Having now examined the opinions of the moſt eminent Writers, that have favoured this *Notion* of a Right in the Britiſh Parliament to *bind* the Subjects of *Ireland* "*when eſpecially named*," I truſt it will appear, to every impartial Reader, that ſuch doctrine is ſo far from having any real *foundation* to ſupport it, that it is really diametrically opposite to some of the most essential *foundations of Law*, and is apparently *subversive* of one of the first principles of the British *Constitution!* so that it will be needless for me to take notice of any thing that has been said to the *same purpose* by inferior Writers, or by the Editors or Collectors of Law Dictionaries, *&c.* who have *only quoted* these great authorities which I have already demonstrated to be *erroneous*; and I may therefore, I hope, be now allowed to repeat with double satisfaction and certainty what I before asserted only upon *general Principles* in the first Part of this Declaration, *viz.* that "*the true constitutional mode of* CONNECTING *British Dominions, that are otherwise separated by* "NATURE, *is demonstrated by the established example of the union of* GREAT "BRITAIN *and* IRELAND, *which by long experience has proved to be sufficiently effectual*," p. 21.

But,

But, notwithſtanding that I have already been led to a tedious length of argument by the neceſſary examination of ſo many authors, I muſt beg leave ſtill to add ſome general remarks upon the above-mentioned groundleſs argument drawn from *the Right of Conqueſt*; for Judge Blackſtone has been equally unguarded in what he has laid down concerning the *American Colonies* in p. 107. of the ſame volume, where he has made a very improper uſe of this ſame miſtaken notion about the Right of Conqueſt.

" Our *American* Plantations" (ſays he) " are principally of this latter ſort," (*viz.* conquered or ceded countries, of which he was treating in the preceding ſentence,) " being obtained" (ſays he) " in " the laſt century, either by RIGHT OF " CONQUEST, *and driving out the Na-* " *tives, (with what natural Juſtice I* " *ſhall not at preſent enquire,) or by Trea-*

 " *ties.*

" *ties. And therefore*" (*says he*) " *the* " COMMON LAW OF ENGLAND, *as* " *such, has no* ALLOWANCE *or authority* " *there*; they being *no part of the mother* " *Country, but distinct (though dependent)* " *Dominions.*" But, when he reconsiders this part of his work, I trust he will allow that the COMMON LAW of *England* is principally founded on *Reason, natural Justice*, and *the eternal Laws of God*; and consequently all that part of the COMMON LAW, which arises from *these foundations*, MUST HAVE " *allowance or* " *authority*," not only *there* (*viz.* in the English Colonies) but *every where else*, if the unjust pretensions of Tyrants were to be duly restrained by *Law* and *Equity*: and, with respect to the *remaining part* of the COMMON LAW, consisting in ancient and approved *usages* and *customs, peculiar to English Subjects*, he will not be backward, I trust, to grant them also " *allowance or authority there*," when he

is

is reminded that these *conquered Countries* are not inhabited by *the conquered People*, but chiefly by *British Subjects*, successors to *the Conquerors*, who are entitled by *Birth-right* to the *Common Law of England*, and every other privilege of Englishmen, quite as much as those *English Subjects* mentioned by him at the top of the same page. "*For it hath been held*," (says he) "*that if an uninhabited country* "*be discovered and* PLANTED BY ENG-"LISH SUBJECTS, ALL THE EN-"GLISH LAWS THEN IN BEING, "*which are the* BIRTH-RIGHT OF "EVERY SUBJECT, *are immediately* "THERE IN FORCE." 1 Com. p. 107. This doctrine is unquestionable; and the more so because allowed by himself: And though he has been pleased to add, that "this *must be understood with* "*very many and very great restrictions*;" that "*such Colonists carry with them only* "*so much of the English Law*, as is ap-"plicable

"plicable to their own ſituation," &c. yet it muſt be apparent that, if they "*carry with them*" any Laws *at all*, it moſt be by virtue of their *natural Right as Engliſhmen*, whereby they are certainly as much entitled *to all*; (I mean all the Engliſh Laws that were in being when theſe ſeveral Colonies reſpectively were eſtabliſhed;) and therefore, though they *uſed* (in the infant ſtate of each Colony) "*only* "*ſo much of the Engliſh Law* as was ap-"plicable to *their own ſituation*," (and it is abſurd to ſuppoſe that they would *uſe* more, whether intitled to it or not,) yet this does not affect their undoubted *Right to the whole*; which *Right* deſcends to poſterity and ſucceſſors in the ſame manner as all other *inheritances*; it being, indeed, their *very beſt inheritance* (78): And Equity ſurely entitles the increaſing Colonies (continually as occaſions

(78) Judge Blackſtone himſelf has called it in the the very ſame page "*the Birth-Right of every Subject.*"

occasions may arise from their improvements) to the use and benefit of *all beneficial Laws* which were in force at the time of their ancestors emigration.

That these, however, "*must be understood with*" *some* "*Restrictions*," cannot be denied;—as the Laws of "*Revenue*," (for instance,) which the learned Gentleman himself has mentioned: for these were merely local, and cannot therefore be *legally* enforced in any new Dominions without the express Assent or Grant of the Inhabitants in such new Dominions, the same being absolutely necessary to give them a *local* effect within the said Dominions: because nothing but the *free Grant* and *Assent* of the *Inhabitants and Landholders* gave them force, *originally*, even in the mother Country; and, therefore, nothing but the *like authority* (that is, the free Grant of *the Inhabitants upon the spot* wherever they are introduced)

introduced) can possibly render them *legal*, *just*, and *binding* in any other part of the world; so that it must necessarily appear, that no new acquired Territories, settled by British Subjects, can *legally* be taxed by English Acts of Parliament, nor be bound thereby in their *internal* Government without such manifest *injustice* and *iniquity* as must necessarily render *null and void* all such pretended Acts; for, otherwise, if they were admitted, they would render all the temporal hereditary possessions and property of the Subjects in the Colonies entirely *uncertain*, which is one of the most odious circumstances in the eye of the Law that can be mentioned. "*Quod certum est retinendum est*, quod INCERTUM "EST *dimittendum:* Nay, *quod* INCERTUM "EST NIHIL EST:" This is the censure of Law upon all the Acts of Men "which fall under the judgement of the "Law. If then THE LAW so judge of "the

" the Acts of Men, HOLDING THEM FOR " NOUGHT and VOYDE that are INCER- " TAINE; how much more then doth " THE LAW REQUIRE CERTAINTY *in* " *her own Acts*, which are to bind all " Men." The Liberty of the Subject against the pretended Power of Impositions, by Wm. Hakewil, 1641.

I have been the more particular (as well here as upon Orurke's case before-mentioned) in expressing the necessity of restraining the *Power of Parliament* within the bounds of *Reason*, *Justice*, and *natural Equity*, because, I find, it is too common an error that an *Act of Parliament is omnipotent*, and that whatever is ordained by Parliament *must be Law*, without any exception of *Right* or *Wrong*, *White* or *Black*, *Truth* or *Falsehood!* which, God be thanked, is very far from being *true*, though the learned Commentator Judge Blackstone, upon the very ſame point, (the *Omnipotence of Parliament,)* has unguardedly ſaid, " *True it* " *is, that what the Parliament doth, no* " *Authority upon earth can undo.*" 1 Com. p. 161. But that worthy Gentleman needs only to be reminded, that if it ſhould unfortunately happen, from any *overſight* or *miſunderſtanding*, that " *what* " *the Parliament doth*" is in the leaſt contrary either to the Laws of Reaſon, Nature, pure Morality, natural Equity and Juſtice ; or to that *Benevolence* (79) and

(79) This *Benevolence*, or due *Conſideration* for the *natural Rights* of all mankind is properly called *Jus Gentium*, the *Law of Nations* ;* which univerſal Law (as

* The Law of Nations ſeems to be almoſt baniſhed at this time from *Europe*. The late felonious and arbitrary Diviſion of Poland between three of the greateſt Powers in Europe : The late iniquitous attempts againſt the antient Republic of Venice and the Swiſs Cantons, and the late unjuſt Claims upon the free Cities of Dantzick, Hamburgh, *&c.* The Robberies and horrid Murders which, for theſe ten years paſt, have been committed by the French on the *poor wretched* Inhabitants of the little Iſland of Corſica, upon pretence of an *unlawful* Ceſſion of Sovereignty from the Genoeſe ; and the like abominable Iniquity, upon the like falſe pretence, lately carried on, even by the *Engliſh* themſelves, againſt the poor helpleſs Charibbs at St. Vincent's : — are melancholy Proofs, either that the Europeans in general are moſt profoundly ignorant of the *Law of Nations*, or that they are fallen into a ſtate of the moſt abandoned Wickedneſs and Profligacy.

and Consideration which we owe, not only to our brethren and countrymen,

Hh 2 but

(as likewise ALL THE OTHER HEADS above-mentioned) is necessarily included in what is commonly called *natural Religion*, consisting of the primary or *eternal Laws* of God; and whatsoever is contrary to any of these is "MALUM IN SE," which no authority on earth can make lawful; (see note in p. 185 & 186.) and *men* of all ranks, and in all places, that have *Common Sense*, are *naturally* qualified to distinguish whether Laws are deficient in any of these respects, or are contrary to *Reason*; for the LAW OF REASON is an universal Law — "*Scribiturque* HÆC LEX *in* "*corde* CUJUSLIBET HOMINIS, *docens eum quid a*-"*gendum, et quid fugiendum*," (for which the learned Author quotes the Epistle to the Romans, chap. 2, and then proceeds) "*et quod* LEX RATIONIS *in corde* "*scribitur, ideo deleri non potest, nec etiam recipit muta*-"*tionem ex loco nec tempore, sed ubique* ET INTER OM-"NES HOMINES *servari debet. Nam* JURA NATU-"RALIA IMMUTABILIA SUNT, *et ratio immutationis* "*est quod recipiunt Naturam rei pro fundamento, quæ* "*semper eadem est et ubique*." Doct. et Stud. cap. 2. Any *Acts of Parliament*, therefore, which are contrary either to *Nature*, to *Justice*, to *Morality*, or to *Benevolence*, &c. are contrary to REASON, (that Ray of the divine Nature, and supreme Law,) and consequently are *null and void*, being mere Corruptions, (*corruptelæ,*) and not Laws; for "*contra eam*" (Rationem) "*non est præscriptio vel appositum statutum sive consue*-"*tudo; et, si aliqua fiat*, NON SUNT STATUTA, "*sive Consuetudines, sed* CORRUPTELÆ," &c. Doct. et Stud. p. 5. b.

but alſo to our *brethren of the univerſe,* by the *ties of nature*; or, 2dly, if contrary to the written Laws of God; (80) or, 3dly, if contrary to any of the *fundamental Rights and Franchiſes* declared in the Great Charter; (81) or, 4thly, if contrary to TRUTH; (that is, if any Act be made upon *partial* information or groundleſs ſuggeſtions, which ſhall have occaſioned

(80) " *Secundum fundamentum legis Angliæ eſt* LEX " DIVINA," &c. And if any Act of Parliament is in any degree contrary to *the divine Law,* it has no force in the Laws of *England.* Suppoſe, for inſtance, an Act of Parliament ſhould be made, to prohibit or annul the marriages of any particular rank or order of men whatſoever; the ſame muſt neceſſarily be eſteemed null and void of itſelf; becauſe the *Principle,* attempted to be eſtabliſhed by ſuch an imaginary Act, is ſo directly *contrary to the Laws of God,* that we may ſafely rank it with the " DOCTRINES OF DEVILS;" (ſee notes on pages 133 & 134.) which, indeed, every Act of Parliament ought to be eſteemed that is in any degree contrary to *the holy Scriptures,* (the written Laws of God,) or contrary to *Reaſon,* (the *eternal Law* of God) — " *Etiam ſi* ALIQUOD STATUTUM *eſſet editum contra eos,* NULLIUS VIGORIS *in legibus Angliæ* " *cenſeri debet,*" &c. Doct. et Stud. c. 6.

(81) Of this I have already given ſufficient examples in pages 178 to 208.

occasioned a misrepresentation of TRUTH in the recital of facts;) (82) if, in any of *these points*, it should unfortunately happen (I say) that "*what the Parliament* "*doth*" is really defective, or made contrary thereto, the same ought to be "HOLDEN FOR NONE!" There needs "*no authority upon earth*" to undo what is *so done*, for it is ***null and void*** of itself, notwithstanding the united authority of King, Lords, and Commons! And, whenever any Acts have been thus inadvertently or too hastily made, the most honourable method of getting rid of them is, by the same authority, to *declare* *them*

(82) "*Contra veritatem nihil possumus.*" And again, "Contra veritatem lex nunquam aliquid per-" mittit." 2 Inst. 252. Plowden has reported a variety of cases wherein Acts of Parliament were esteemed *void in Law*, through the want of *truth* in the recitals: see pages 398 to 400. — "Et issint "Parliament puit missprender chose, et Statutes que "MISRECITE CHOSES, et sont referre a eux, SER-"RONT VOID, et null serra conclude per eux. Issint "en notre principal case, le statut que recite le plain-"tiff fuit attaint, et confirme ceo, ou en fail il ne "fuit attaint, SERRA VOIDE."

them null and void, and not merely to *re-peal* them, because the latter is not a sufficient reparation to *injured justice and truth*; for, as all men are fallible, it is disingenuous and highly dishonourable, in any man, or body of men whatsoever, not to acknowledge a *mistake* or *error*, when the same is fairly demonstrated!

" *The power and jurisdiction of the* " *Parliament, for making of Laws*," &c. is NOT therefore " *so transcendent and* " *absolute that it cannot be confined, either* " *for causes or persons*," (as supposed by Lord Coke, 4 Inst. p. 36,) " *within* " *any bounds*," since the just *bounds* and limits of it are so very clearly defined, as well as the due bounds of *regal Power*, that they fall within the judgement of every man who has COMMON SENSE to distinguish GOOD from EVIL, or RIGHT from WRONG; so that the imaginary OMNIPOTENCE OF PARLIAMENT is not only

only (as Judge Blackſtone has declared) "*a figure rather too bold*;" but even totally falſe and unjuſt; becauſe the Parliament is manifeſtly limited, (as all powers on earth muſt be,) and CANNOT "*do every thing that is not* NATURALLY "*impoſſible*;" though Judge Blackſtone ſuppoſes it can (1 Com. p. 161.) for the "POWER (83) OF RIGHT (or Juſtice) "alone is of GOD; but that of WRONG "(or Injury) is of the DEVIL; and "the works of whichſoever of theſe "the King" (or any other man) "ſhall "do, of the ſame ſhall he be eſteemed "the ſervant." (84)

So

(83) —— "Quia illa poteſtas" (poteſtas Juris) "ſolius Dei eſt; poteſtas autem injuriæ diaboli, et "non Dei; et cujus horum opera fecerit rex, ejus "miniſter erit cujus opera fecerit. Igitur, dum facit juſtitiam, vicarius eſt Regis æterni; miniſter "autem diaboli, dum declinet ad injuriam," &c. Bracton, lib. 3, c. 9, p. 107 b.

(84) "Know ye not that, to whom ye yield your"ſelves *ſervants* to obey, *his ſervants* ye are, to whom "ye obey? whether of ſin unto death, or of obedi"ence unto righteouſneſs?" &c. Rom. vi. 16.

So that "*the Powers that be*" cannot bind the conſcience when they exceed *juſt limits*, any more than the threats of a *lawleſs Banditti*; and therefore we may truly ſay *of all the Branches of the Legiſlature together*, (I mean their united authority,) what the ingenious Mr. Sadler ſaid particularly concerning the Houſe of Commons; *viz.* "*When they are* FREE-"EST, *they have* LIMITS; *for they be* "*not infinite. Nay, when they are* MOST "FREE, *they are* MOST BOUND *to* GOOD "ORDERS, *and to* RIGHT-REASON." Sadler's Rights, p. 135.

It would be happy for this kingdom if all Members of Parliament were ſenſible of theſe *indiſpenſible limitations*; and therefore, though I have thought it my duty to oppoſe what Judge Blackſtone has unfortunately allowed concerning the imaginary OMNIPOTENCE OF PARLIAMENT,

PARLIAMENT, yet I think myſelf bound moſt heartily to concur with him in what he has mentioned in the ſame page — 'That it is a matter moſt eſſential to 'the liberties of this kingdom, that 'ſuch members be delegated to this 'important Truſt, as are moſt emi- 'nent for their probity, their fortitude, 'and their knowledge; for it was a 'known apophthegm of the great Lord 'Treaſurer Burleigh, "that England "could never be ruined but by a Par- "liament," *&c.*

But, before I conclude this 2d part of my Declaration, it may, perhaps, be expected that I ſhould apologize for the tedious length of it; and yet, when my Readers conſider that it was neceſſary for me to anſwer the aſſertions of ſome of the moſt eminent Law Writers that this nation, perhaps, ever produced, they will not think their time ill ſpent (I hope) in following me through this minute examination of the ſaid aſſertions, eſpecially as they relate to the moſt *important points of the* CONSTITUTION *and* COMMON LAW *of England and Ireland.*

And I hope, alſo, that my Readers will not charge me *with preſumption*, for having, in the courſe of this argument, oppoſed the opinions of ſuch very reſpectable Writers as *Baron Puffendorf* on THE CIVIL LAW, and *the Judges Coke, Vaughan, Jenkins, and Blackſtone*, and *the Hon. Mr. Barrington, on* THE LAWS OF ENGLAND. If my Remarks ſhould, in any part, be thought too ſevere, I am ſorry for it: I can only aſſure my Readers that the leaſt *perſonal diſreſpect* is not intended; for I am ſufficiently ſenſible of my own unworthineſs and *too ſuperficial knowledge in all things*; and have, therefore, moſt carefully avoided any doctrine which may ſeem to reſt merely upon the weak foundation

dation of my own opinion; but, whereever I have ventured to diſſent from the opinions of theſe approved writers, I have aſſigned plain *reaſons* for it, or other *proper authorities*, and I deſire to be truſted no farther than theſe *plain reaſons* and *authorities* will fairly warrant. I hope I may be permitted to uſe the ſame apology for pointing out miſtakes in the opinions of theſe very learned writers which the *Hon. Mr. Juſtice Barrington* has applied particularly to the Inſtitutes and Reports of *Sir Edward Coke*; which "*being*" (ſays he) "*the* "*beſt* LAW-CHART, *and implicitly truſted* "*to, it is proper to take notice of every* "*ſhoal and rock miſplaced, though per-* "*haps not in the proper track of naviga-* "*tion,*" p. 91.

GRANVILLE SHARP.

"LEX *plus laudatur quando* RATIONE "*probatur.*" Co. Lit. Epil.

" *Post varios casus, post tot discrimina*
" *rerum,*
" *Nunc sequitur conclusio.*"

(Soli) " DEO GLORIA ET GRATIA."

" *Jucunda est præteritorum laborum*
" *memoria.*" 2 Inst. Epil.